Memoirs from the War in Heaven

by
John H. Doe
Herald of The Lord Jesus Christ

a.k.a.
Sir Michael of the Candle
Knight of the Narrow Way

Cover: Gustave Moreau, *The Travelling Poet*

Copyright © 2014 by John H. Doe

All rights reserved.

No part of this book may be reproduced or transmitted in any form by any means, mechanical or electronic, including recording or photocopying, by any type of information storage or retrieval system, except as is expressly permitted by the 1976 Copyright Act or by written permission from the author.

1 And There Was Light

Late repentance is seldom true, but true repentance is never too late.

– Ralph Venning

What was before this? What was before the beginning? It comes not at first thought—we usually focus on what is presented, from the beginning on. But upon the introspection, we wonder what happened before it all happened. We find even before the original beginning, in fact, before "In the beginning," it turns out there was not nothing, not even way back there; not empty was the void at all—not completely. I had thought that, too, you know, that it was creation *ex nihilo*: out of nothing. When I did hear what had been there, it opened some doors of thought, what such circumstance might have spelled.

If you read carefully, Genesis said that the Earth was formless and void, and what I found that this meant was that before all things existed was a primordial chaos. To the Babylonians, this was symbolized by the monster Tiamat. In the Old Testament, the beast of that chaos was named Rahab. In the old myths, the progenitor god slays the beast of the chaos and from the body is formed the world that is. We can see that myths themselves change, but there seems to be a deep memory that we share of the old things of the world.

Note that the term "chaos" may be misleading. One may think of things flying around randomly, electric like or a sandstorm. It was nothing like that. Think, instead, of a watery goop, with little, if any, definition at all. When I heard that description of what it was supposed to be like, I had in my head that perhaps the chaos may have been the remnants of a previous creation, after it had attained a heat death: maximal entropy. Perhaps not, but that was a not unworthy speculation. Whatever this formless mush may be likened to be, it was as if from out of this that God made the heaven and the earth. And out of the darkness He said, "Let there be light." And there was light.

There is also a very interesting line that is written in the book of Revelation, almost completely without context: after calling Jesus Christ the Lamb, it says he was the Lamb slain at the foundation of the world. It brings us back from the end of the Bible back to the beginning again. I think it tells us a thing or so about how time may work, for this speaks of an event in eternity. But we'll return to this idea. For now, suffice it that (outside of eternity) there was at the beginning, God—and the Word was God—plus the primordial chaos. Which, if you think about it, doesn't really seem to be the type of stuff that God would make. There is perhaps another story there, another myth at work. And you know what they say about myths: they are lies that tell the truth.

This book is about a myth, of which very little is written of in authoritative sources: the War in Heaven. Jesus Christ mentioned it once, saying that he saw Satan falling from Heaven like lightning. And in Revelation, it says that Satan and his angels were forced out of the place above by Michael and his angels. That's pretty much it. There is supplemental material, of course, the most notable being Milton's *Paradise Lost,* but that is about as reliable as Dante's account of the *Inferno,* the *Purgatorio,* and the *Paradiso.* These weren't prophets, as far as anyone knows, or that they claim.

Insofar as it relates to my own circumstance, the events of the War directly impacted the life I lived. I write from experience, not imagination, though you may be tempted to think that at times my imagination ran away with me.

As it happened, the beginning for me—where anything like a saga begins in my life—that would be October 7, 1988, at Carnegie Mellon University, Pittsburgh. I was 19 and invincible and heavily into dropping acid at the time. There had been floating around the circles I haunted of this LSD from Georgia, which had a print off a Grateful Dead album on it. We called it the "Dead acid". In other words, its name was a warning. People were having bad trips on it; it was too strong, maybe there was strychnine in it. I of course got my hands on some. By that time, I was already doing multiple hits every time I tripped, which came down to a schedule of about once every weekend.

So I told everybody I was going to take 5 hits of it. I had planned on trying 5 sometime and what the heck? This sounded like a fun time to follow through. People were like, "No, don't! Take a half a tab, see what it's like first." OK, so maybe I did listen a little, was a little bit afraid, I suppose. I told them I was going to take 3, then. "No, don't! Try a half a tab…" So I took 3 hits. I had taken 3 hits of a strong acid before; I figured, what's the worst that could possibly happen? Even now having something of a gut feeling that this was going to be one for the books. And I knew almost immediately after taking those 3 tabs that this was not going to be your regular hallucinogenic experience.

Usually it takes about a half hour to start tripping, but as 20 minutes cut in, I was already tripping *hard*. I thought to call my friend Bob and told him I was losing touch with reality, and he said, "We'll be right over." I remember watching the patterns flow over the carpet waiting for them to show up. Indeed, my regular group of stoner friends came over, and we were hanging out in my dorm room, and of course, we were passing around a bong. There I was, sitting on my bed—the cause for concern that night—taking hits from the bong, basically unable to speak. I simply forgot how to make that leap in functionality.

There were other people who were tripping, and they seemed as if to glow in comparison to the normals. I wondered if the ones tripping could also see that. Then my mother called, and my roommate answered; he looked at me and saw that I was not capable of anything like regular conversation and so he said to her, "He's not here." Which did something psychological to me. (I was nowhere: I was not but lies. And one thing I would learn, through all these experiences: the madness has a memory.) She said she would call back at 9. I might say that it really started right then, my descent into the Dark Wood… to be followed by my ascent out beyond.

I remember some things about what came next, in small vignettes, disconnected, confused. I think they took me for a walk at some point, when I was making absolutely no sense. I'm not sure I was speaking real English in the snatches of conversation that I seem to recall. When I was in my room, not sure if that was before or after the trip outside, and I remember sitting in my dorm room, and the smell of when someone knocked over the bong. Pungent, if you know the smell of "fresh" bongwater.

Maybe this was it, what really sent me over the top: right after I exited the bathroom, which was semi-private, shared with the room next door, my friend Aaron asked me how I was doing, which was nothing in itself, but then he made a gesture with his eyebrows, innocent like a playful, "Hm?" and WHAM! (I understood later that people tripping actually had battles twitching their eyebrows in such provocative manners.) Right then, I had a satori—an awakening—which was like a SATORI, such a rush, but terribly twisted: a sudden realization that I had been so whacked out on drugs they had put me into a drug rehab center without my knowing, which the current reality actually was, and now I was being awakened, finally, to know what was REALLY going on, that my parents and such were waiting for me on the outside. And now, that I was aware of what was the underlying reality, I needed to get out. Get OUT.

The theme, you could say, was waking up. I went out my door into the hallway and I saw the exit sign at the opposite end, and I started running to it. Out! Out! Of course, there happened to be a set of double doors midway down the hall, which, since I could see through their windows, I think I assumed I would run right through them, apparently just like light. So, I literally *ran* into those doors, face first. I was knocked for a loop. I was floored. I chipped a tooth. I had this vision and thought I saw this guy who dropped out the semester before walk across the ceiling. That had been a guy named Sam, who freaked out while tripping on a bunch of acid while at home winter break. And then things become scattered vignettes again.

I think Bob went out to find me, and actually, was *this* when they took me for the walk? Confused, that whole sequence of happening. Because I remember it was three of us, though I also remember just me and Bob when we had the nonsensical conversation. But there we were, three of us, when we were outside the dorm and they hinted that someone had the keys to get in. And I picked up on it! I was beginning to get a clue. Waking up to reality. The way things work. You know, sense and sanity. Then we went upstairs, back to my room, now evacuated. Innocently, I asked Bob what time it was, and he said, "9 o'clock." And then WHAM! In a rush: my mom going to call me at 9, parents waiting for me outside, the drug rehab center, everything was FAKE! I ran out again, pushing my way through the double doors in the middle of the hall now, out the back door of my dorm, and I said, dramatically, "I'm off drugs!"

I ran down the stairs, and down a driveway where there was a big EXIT sign, and running, staring at the word "EXIT". And something quite remarkable started to happen: I began to lose contact with my body. Seriously, like my soul were coming loose, the connection between me inside and what was staring at the word, "EXIT"; and my legs running began to come loose, and in the space of a few seconds, I lost control of my body completely. So I fell, and skidded on the asphalt. That was the *beginning* of the weirdness, if you haven't had enough yet.

As my body lay there, I became a completely loose freeform entity. I passed *down,* through layers of consciousness, I saw the connections to how we come to perceive the world around us, then where the symbols we use were grounded, and then completely OUT of my body, so that I was a pure sphere. A sphere, but whose whole surface was an eye: I could see out in all directions without having to turn my head (as if that were the issue, since I had no body parts at all)—but where was I? Part of me, the spherical eye, could see where I had just been, the hallway of my dorm and the door and the exit sign above it. Was this it then, the exit I had been looking for?

I got a little scared. Mostly from confusion, plus the absolute strangeness of what had just happened. And then appeared there before me two of my friends, but I knew they weren't really my friends, rather that these two beings were symbols of all that was right and good about the cosmos, of heaven and earth. One of them said, "John, this is the only reality you've got. Up, up!" And I knew exactly what I needed to do. I wonder now if anyone else had visited where I had been, and were not able to get back. Would they have been catatonic? Would it have been a coma state? I was lucky, and with that cue, "Up, up!", I passed back up *through* my layers of consciousness, *back* into my body, and I stood up. I started walking back up the driveway, saying, "I love this place, Hunt Library..." Then I saw Bob coming down the stairs.

All he said when he saw me was, "John, where are you going?" But I was having none of it. Because he was a symbol of that which was below, the darkness, of all that was wrong, the drug rehab center and the fake reality I was trying to wake up from, trying to escape. Ironic that he had come because he was concerned about me. So, as my state of mind had determined the course I was to follow, I veered right and ran away, yelling, "I'm off drugs!" Later Bob told me this only added to my legend, and that I was a particularly fast runner. But where was I going, actually?

I had it in my mind to get out of this fake reality/drug rehab center, and I had a vision of a fall. I had decided that whatever it took, however it would feel, I was going to *get out*. So I was making a beeline (if bees turned 90 degree corners) to Schenley Bridge, about 100 feet high off the ground, midway—to jump off it.

And then what happened was the best thing ever. This was worth the price of admission, and a half. I was running up this hill, and I heard a voice inside my head say something like, if you want to get out, you'll have to run forever! And this maze appeared in my mind, extending beyond my vision's reach, and I was supposed to fill it with my running. Short hesitation while still running full throttle, when I decided, "Yes!" And at that instant, there opened a white light in the maze, the middle of my imagination; and when I tried to wrap my mind around it, the white light completely overtook me, and now was there nothing but the light, so bright as to be solid, more solid than steel or diamond whatever you could find in any earthly realm—and it was as if I did not exist in comparison to the light, and I was told I was not that light. It was then my perception closed upon it: the circle whose center is everywhere, its circumference nowhere: INFINI-

TY. And I was dropped back into my body, which had fallen for a second time onto the pavement.

As soon as I perceived what I could of it, it let me go. But the thing was: I felt I had gotten out. Ha! I didn't realize what was going on there until much later. That the forces of evil were directing me to go and kill myself, but basically had no chance of getting that done. For I had a destiny to fulfill. After perceiving that light, I didn't need to jump off the bridge anymore. I was awake. I had been rescued, from out of nowhere, *ex nihilo:* out of nothing. There had been nothing in the way between the asphalt where I decided to go and jump from life, and the bridge where I was going to do it. I was saved. In fact, I had no idea *how* saved I actually was.

And the story continues. I got up from being sprawled on the sidewalk, sort of dazed, and I walked around to the front of Hunt Library and saw this girl passerby, and I guess I must have thought, she'll do. I told her, with my finger pointing at her, in no uncertain terms, "I don't care who you are, I want you to call my mother and tell her I'm off drugs!" Yes, this is what made sense to me just then. It was my version of being thankful, I think. She looked at me as one might expect, as if I were the old meaning of the word, "queer," and I hope I didn't scare her too bad, and she walked off.

I guess she must have told someone about that little encounter because as I swung around to the back of the building, two big ROTC guys (perhaps Marines) found me and tackled me and held me down. I forget if they tried to talk to me or each other… At that time, I remembered the martial arts I took in high school. Not that I've ever been violent to anyone but myself, no matter how insane I ever got. Thank the Lord for that. But I did think, *I can get out of this hold.* And I could almost see the pathway out, and 1, 2, 3, twisted myself free. As I walked away, Carnegie

Mellon security showed up in their little squad car. And that was a thing I wasn't going to try and escape from, for the moral dimension had I been bound to, this whole trip. I dropped to the ground. *Busted.* The security guy cuffed me and asked for my name, and I said, "John Doe". "Yeah, right." "ID, back pocket." "What do you know." Then he asked me what drugs I was on, and I said, "Acid, 3 hits". And then I suppose he called for an ambulance, because one came.

I don't recall the ambulance ride. I remember arriving at the hospital. I was restrained. I vaguely recall the catheter being put in. (I certainly remember when they took it out!) There was an orderly next to my bed. As I said, I was restrained, but I could sit up. And every time I did, spouting this or that nonsense from the world according to drugs, the orderly shoved me back down. And maybe it might have been that they sedated me, because I went to sleep. I certainly was past the peak of my trip. Hallucinating lightly, staring up at the ceiling, I drifted off.

When I woke up, I was all, "Where am I?" "Why is my lip bloody?" (Where I chipped my tooth.) "Why am I tied down?" "What happened?" And about then, Bob showed up with my other friend, Boris. Boris hadn't really been there before, but was just concerned about me. I suppose the news had already started spreading. And I must admit it must have gone over pretty well. It was not like I was a newbie tripper, and I end up in a hospital. I once heard the description of that night from Bob's point of view. He said, we heard that John was admitted to Presby so we decided to go down and see how he was doing. As we were being led to where he was being kept, we weren't sure if he was still gone or not. But when we got to his bed, he turned and looked at us and said, "That was wild!" And we knew he was back.

I tried for the rest of that semester to regain the one part of that trip: the infinite light. I kept tripping every weekend, did 10 hits at once two weekends in a row. Nothing. (Well, not nothing—a trip, but never that Light. Not ever again. Stuff like the floor liquefying, walls melting, etc., etc.) I thought about that Light, later on, and I thought about it a lot: it was the aspect of ultimate action, running as hard as I possibly could, my unequivocal, "Yes!"—it was the ultimate experience of Yang. (And in fact, some years later I experienced the ultimate Yin, but we'll get to that.) And yes, as you might well think: that was God. The trim of God's light, the barest taste of the Glory. One might take the belief that one could not behold the Glory of God and live, and take this new tack on it—a human soul would not be able to withstand it, blown away into nothing if it were to happen. The vision of Him was expressed in terms I could understand: not just Yang, but two other aspects I experienced: God is light, God is love. I had gotten out, escaped the *maya*. My life was saved, in this world and the next. And more: this was when and how I was drafted as a soldier in the War in Heaven, though I did not understand that until much, much later. This was my beginning. Of the Purpose I was born for. This was to be my defining moment for years to come.

There's an interesting thing about this beginning. In February and March of 1974 (he called it 2-3-74; mine I call 10/7/88), Philip K. Dick had a series of mystical experiences which would consume his attention for the last 8 years of his life. He would go on to write 8,000 handwritten pages about them, what he called his Exegesis. And a couple three years ago, they published a good clip of it, and it came out to about 1,000 pages, printed. What makes all this interesting is that, as far as the editor(s) report, on the very last page of what Dick jotted down before he died, he wrote, "The Yang side is the bright unfallen side and in salvador salvandus, one's other—and rational—self, who enters in order to rescue the Yin or limited or darkened, incarnated side."[i] So, in other words,

I picked up exactly where he left off: his end, my beginning. The "Yang side" that rescued me as I was running to my death. What a co-inkydink.

Indeed, I didn't remember until years later a vision I had right after the infinite light, when I was plopped back into my body. I saw a cosmic egg split in two, one pink half and one light blue half, and I saw the light blue part enter me in my imagination, while the pink part went off elsewhere. Why this matters: Philip K. Dick saw a blinding pink light in the 2-3-74 experiences. So this was a clue that I was looking into eternity, as mentioned before. I was seeing in my timeline where it (at least at this point) intersected with Phil's, way back 14 years previous. Yes, time is strange when viewed with hints from eternity.

I also would understand further that the two actually were red and blue essences, infused with light. And further still: Phil wrote that he felt the presence of a twin that had come into contact with 2-3-74, whom he had a bunch of theories about (along with everything else, of course), a twin whom he called Thomas (the name meaning "twin"). Putting 2 and 2 together, I recognized that I *am* that Thomas. Or maybe 2 and 1.5 together and rounding up: the description of Thomas is almost nothing like me. Only once does he write that Thomas might be in the future, and at other intervals he places Thomas back in Apostolic times, right after they crucified the J-man. But really, there is no other explanation: I am that twin, the twin of Philip K. Dick, I who was tuned to pick up where he left off, to finish our mission here on Earth. Crazy enough for you yet? Welcome to my world.

I should have known everything had changed from 10/7/88, because the type of acid trips I started having were substantively different. Someone or something had (re)organized my mind. How I looked at everything in the world had changed. Most only in subtle ways, but in retrospect I noticed how things were now as if catalogued when I was tripping. Surely the hand of the former twin. They all began to have an overarching theme to them; they were all of a certain superparadigm. Before, as I would come down from a trip, it would be things like imagining a weird game show type aesthetic as I fell asleep—quite naïve/immature. After, the trips were about Heaven and Hell, sin and salvation, being lost and being found. And sometimes reality could be explained in terms of the trip, and be a lesson indeed.

For instance, one friend said he was the Antichrist, and there was this (was it a dream?) image in which a supernal voice (the Lord?) talked about me to another higher-up (Mother Nature?) saying something like, "Look at that, he's friends with the Antichrist now." Apparently, not a good sign, someone trying to tell me something about my life. These were me picking up from where my twin left things, gone 6 years before the date of my encounter with God. The Light had no message for me then, but my, would that change.

10/7/88 would be the superpattern of my life for years. For *years*. I would relate any important event that happened to where in the course of the 10/7/88 experience it seemed to echo from. When I ran from the room? When I lost contact with my body? When I thought of suicide? And at points I would come under mental duress, and if it involved the mention of drugs, the twisted satori that creation were a big drug rehab center would rear its so very weird visage. I would only be free from that 7 years and thousands of miles away from its source, when I heard a voice and saw the hint of a man's face say to me, something like, "Hey, you can go now." I knew that that could only mean one thing. It was one of those types of freedom that afterwards, one easily forgets. As it only restored the normal, because of that, one needs never to think of it again.

That beginning was my sophomore year of college. I practically didn't go to one class that year, and my grades showed it. They were so bad that I was kicked out for the following year, called academic suspension. Oy, my parents were upset about that. I did get a job then, and was relatively productive as a member of society. I didn't drop acid that frequently, did smoke pot a lot driving around with my friend Steve, a fellow stoner. We ate a lot of Roy Rogers chicken. I couldn't wait to get back to school though. The suburbs were smotheringly boring. I called it Purgatory, where I longed instead for Heaven and Hell. And I had had my glimpse of Heaven. Time to look at the other place….

2 Exploded View

I found the rabbit hole goes down fast, and that it goes down deep. As far as knowing that that was where I was headed down, I was no Alice. I needed no white rabbit to follow, to fall in all by lonesome. And here came junior year. Back to dropping acid every weekend in my single apartment room at Hampshire Hall, off campus but college run. And it was there that the ubertrip started kicking in, the trip that all other trips were just branches of. And it came with the darkness.

This one time, I was beginning to psychedelicize and was looking through some interesting subversive material in the form of *The Book of the SubGenius;* when I was about to snicker about something therein, I happened upon the words, "Don't Laugh," and wow: the Conspiracy had suddenly infiltrated. Like my mind were being read by nefarious forces. I was listening to the radio, but what I heard now was some simplistic tune-like simulation, not real music but an aping of what music was in reality. And I could swear the "song" lyrics were talking to me, or about me. Trips don't normally go like this, folks. I looked out the window: holy crap on a stick! Where did these bars outside my window come from? WTF is outside?!? This isn't Pittsburgh! This isn't Earth! I got the sense that my room were one small cell in an immense building, shut off from everything. I had been transported, somehow, *elsewhere.*

The sky was dim with red, and was there an oppressive presence of something above we didn't want the attention of. (We dared not whisper the word, "evil.") All the buildings were black, a landscape the likes of which I had never seen before. Alien. Like the ancient crossed with the future in architecture, and sinister, iron tortured into the shape of claws at the joints. Black, all black everywhere. Other people had seen this place too: they called it the Black Iron Prison.

That was the first time I thought I had been removed to another dimension, but it was certainly not to be the last. That first time, I believed I had literally died and had gone to Hell. It was Hell. Not that I was in any pain, but the sensation, the atmosphere was exactly how Dante put it: abandon all hope, ye who enter here. The land of utter despair. I imagined how they in the waking world were finding my body. I had thought that I had leaned too far back and crashed my head against the glass, so uncoordinated I had been in my wasted state. So this was going to be my eternity? It was as if my room had been taken with me in it and installed in the netherworld. In the bad place.

That year, one of my posters was Hieronymus Bosch's *Garden of Earthly Delights,* hanging up right above my bed; and on one of my stays in the 'Prison, I looked at the face of the Tree Man in the third panel (which was entitled, "Hell"), and I knew that *that* was where I was. Bosch had seen it too, apparently. If you look in the rear of that panel, *there* was that immense building where I had been prisoner. I did happen to get out all the times I was there, 3 maybe 4 times, and there were some weird productions on how that was accomplished each of those times, but it was the very last time which was the most interesting.

Once again, I looked out the window to that alien expanse. Black? Check. Iron? Check. Prison? Check. I didn't feel worried in the least. Completely old hat. I was sitting in my chair, I think it was, doing something on my computer. (How exactly was it Hell when I had a working Macintosh IIci?) Then came a voice, a whisper, that let me in on the joke, told me the secret to it *all*: "Walt Disney is God." And with that, BOOM! Not just me was it that were freed from the 'Prison, but *everyone* was now free, according to the landscape I could see with my mind's eye, my eye into Halospace. (That was the beginning, I later realized, of the free floating apparitions of people, living and dead, whom I would interact with.) Note that this trip, too, I would come down from, but my psyche was by then quite tweaked. I was more LSD than man.

I had a messiah complex going pretty strong during those days, and definite delusions of grandeur propping up my attitude. Friends described me later as being rather annoying, not caring in conversation what was going on with those friends' lives, and instead it was me me me in Wonderland that I would always go on about. If maybe I had quit taking drugs, right then, *maybe* I would have fully "recovered" and would have went on to live a normal life. No chance. I kept taking trips, out to the strange lands of imagination, and on one of those trips that followed, I wouldn't come back.

It would take a looooong time before I would learn just what it was that I had been caught up in. Almost twenty-five years from what I called the beginning, 10/7/88, if you wanted to know just how long. And I was the lucky one, because Philip K., my compatriot, never knew what was happening to him. All part of the plan though.

Hearken: "And there was war in heaven: Michael and his angels fought against the dragon; and the dragon fought and his angels, And prevailed not; neither was their place found any more in heaven." [Revelation 12:7-8 KJV] That's practically all that was written about the Event itself in the Bible, but of course, in Revelation, even Jesus Christ's life on Earth is summarized into a few sentences. But this was what exactly I joined on 10/7/88, as the twin of Philip K. Dick, after the Light Infinite saved my life: the War in Heaven. A war between angels, and all the host of Heaven were thick in the fray. A war in eternity. At stake: the totality of creation itself. Could it have been anything less?

To understand what was going on, we start with the famous author and Christian J. R. R. Tolkien; not with his more famous works, but the beginning of a mythology he created: a part called the "Ainulindalë", which means, "music of the Ainur". It is his very own creation myth, where everything is formed into its own shape by music. So, we go back to the beginning again, but as it is that we're dealing with Eternity, what is the beginning is not as straightforward as one might imagine. Things often seem to go out of order, and some things seem to happen backwards. For instance, I've already told you about the pink and blue lights and so the intersection between 1974 and 1988.

In the "Ainulindalë", Ilúvatar, who is God, creates angel-like entities known as the Ainur, and they commence to forming all that is to be by way of holy music. But the greatest of the Ainur, Melkor, laid into the ground of creation his own themes, not those purposed by Ilúvatar. Sound familiar? Yes, the brightest one rebelled. Of course, Melkor's musics were not like those of Ilúvatar: one could say that they were like of discord, and not of harmony, not like the others who followed the will of the One. But the situation having so been, we might possibly say all that was wrong with the world came from the themes of Melkor. And when I considered that, I thought to myself how interesting (and rather convenient) it would be if that were true of this, our world—that an evil force were at the heart of all the world's faults, its calamities. But as with many things that make perfect sense, I dismissed the notion offhand.

What if, though? What if, for one, angels had a hand in the way that things are? In the book of Job, God relates that the sons of God (angels) rejoiced in the creation of the world—so they were definitely around at the time. What if, then? What if the Lucifer myth is true, and the greatest of the angels rebelled, swelled up with pride, and caused "a third of the stars"[ii] to be fallen with him? A third of all the angels? *Billions?* What if the "machinery" of Heaven were made so existence could be so bent of purpose, *that far* to the will of the Devil, that it allowed him the invention of pain? That the command base of Lucifer while he was in Heaven could possibly ruin *any idea* of fair play being fair enough? Because this was what it meant to be the greatest being outside of God, in a place where *anything* was possible. To be the prime cause of the all the injustice which we see in the world—for injustice to be, if not the rule, one looming theme: it would be a *big deal.* And now you might guess why he and his legions had to be kicked out. Else the world we live in now would have been worse that you could possibly imagine. Because this just might be the way things work, and worked, way back and now, in the time scales of eternity.

Yeah, I wasn't thinking about any of those things after junior year, though. I did too much drugs, dropped too much acid. Usually I would go back to the parents' place in the summer, where acid was a lot less convenient, to get and to do. Give my mind a rest, right? But no, got a place for the summer in Pittsburgh, and continued on my blissful way to ruin. One trip I did 5 hits and watched *Who Framed Roger Rabbit?* And I wrote down "Walt Disney is God," as if it were gospel truth on the face of it. Of course, I wouldn't get the nuanced take on the saying for 22 more years. And after tripping and tripping, my mind just exploded or something, somewhere along the "high"way.

There were people I could see in my imagination, in my mind's eye, who were not just people one normally imagines in the course of the day. I now don't remember how a normal mind works as far as images appearing in it work. My imagination is still a cavern that seems to extend beyond the confines of my brain's dimensions. These new visions I was having, then, in contact with these people… they had minds of their own, it seemed, some friends, some not so friendly. Philip K. Dick was there, but we were hardly even acquaintances then. And I saw Joan of Arc, too. She was trembling at first sight, but I also saw that she was full of courage. Things had happened to make my mind explode, too, that I had not control of: the War in Heaven had come in force, a couple of times. And this had been a battle wound. A very fortunate wound, I would later see.

    I was an addict at the time, and not much else. College was for me not a place for higher education, at least, not that kind of higher. It had instead been an excuse to live in party central, to be wasted all the time and have no responsibilities at all. When you live that kind of life, there's a big possibility that you will get *messed up*. It was bad. But I did have the presence of mind, after my parents picked me up that summer, to take a leave of absence from school. That happened to be a very *very* good thing, because I wouldn't be back for 5 years. There was no way I was going to go back that fall semester. I was barely able to communicate with anyone.

    It was a few days after my twenty-second birthday when the parents came and got me from the apartment in Pittsburgh and brought me "home". They had told me they were coming, but it completely slipped my mind. With my mind exploding and all that. When they took me back to Havertown, my old home town, I plopped down in my old room and spent the days talking to the people in my head. Not that they showed themselves full of form, like they were in the room with me. They resembled cartoons, and were not fully human in shape. As in, just the face I could see, most of the time, or something like a head and one of their arms. Sometimes the whole body, very infrequent. They were spirits.

    I would have a few theories about who or what I was looking at, the main one that I thought was that these were the people who you see in dreams: my dream mechanism had ruptured, and these were the spillouts. I saw some who were dead, some very much alive. There had been times while on acid I would speak with spirit folk, but they'd be gone when I came down: this was rather permanent. I was on a permanent acid trip. They may have diagnosed me with your conventional mental illnesses of the day, but the buck really just stopped at that: I was on a psychedelic journey that kept going after the usual 8 hours that a well behaved trip ended at. Sometimes it would get better, especially when they found the right medication for me; and sometimes it would get worse, usually if I didn't take said medication. But it was just that I wasn't coming down from this trip, was the long and short of it.

And then there was this thing where I remember I became quite infatuated with Rosanna Arquette. I drove to New York City a couple times when she said she was going to meet me there. Wild goose chases, but it was fun being out of my mind and driving the streets of Manhattan. She came into the picture when I saw an image of her on a videotape box at the local video rental place. I was just walking by, a chance encounter, as these things are sometimes. Right? And why wouldn't I have been immediately infatuated with her? She was the prettiest. (As it said on Eris' apple, "Kallisti!")

My dad, they told me, let out a huge sigh of relief when I turned on the stereo they had installed in my room. It had been in his room before. (Ever should I be thankful for the parents that I had been given. At one point, I realized: no one will ever love you like they do. They do things like giving you the best musical experience in the house.) Of course, I didn't listen to music in any normal way. There were hidden meanings all throughout, ciphers that whispered, mysteries that enveloped you with the tune, death and forever[iii] in the breathing of the notes. I was saved and damned, sometimes, because of the music. Sometimes both in one song. My favorite tune going around was "Painless" by Baby

Animals. I was quite afraid of pain at this point, so it was a theme for the paradise I was going to usher in as the new messiah. I didn't realize that the world had already been saved.

I knocked around my parents' house for a few months, at every chance to get drugs or mooch drugs off friends. Mostly pot. Here's an addict's behavior for you: I started to sell stuff. Books, to start with, and then the whole comic book collection my brother and I had collected from elementary school through senior high. (I would later make it up to him by buying him a new computer, when I had money to spare.) I also found and sold all the silver coins my dad had collected when he was working in retail (his own stores). Maybe I should have shopped around for that little sale, because I remember getting a pittance for them, truly. (I also made up for this by giving him a gold coin, years later—an ounce of gold.) And I never knew where you go to sell your blood, because I surely would have gone and done that. These were pre-GPS days, where people still needed to know where things were before they set off to go there.

It was lying in my old bed, the bed I had slept in from age 8 through 17, where I happened upon the ultimate expression of Yin, to go along with that Yang that saved my life. I had my eyes closed, looking at the internal "landscape" I had grown relatively accustomed to, now. And then, at the left outer edge of my internal vision, this overdude, who seemed to identify himself as Walt Disney (it wasn't him), basically rolled close the door to all my senses, all at once, murmuring something like, "What a pity you thought a woman could be the messiah," along the way. Made absolutely no sense. And then everything went black. Absolute black everything. For a few seconds, at least. Then it was as if someone lifted away the stone, from the right outer edge, and I recognized who it was: Jesus! My heart leapt in joy for a second. And then he was gone, and I was left to go my merry way. Or not so merry. I spent these years after the mind exploded mostly unhappy.

    I did get better, bit by bit, day by day. There were still people in my head, but I could carry on a conversation without trailing off and having to deal with things going on within myself. (Right after my mind had exploded, exchanges with my friends usually included, "John? I asked you a question like 5 minutes ago…") I got a job back with that engineering company I had worked at during my academic suspension between my sophomore and junior years. But it was not the same. They once offered to pay for the rest of college if I stayed on with them. Now I was merely a competent worker. Sure, I could still function, but my star had faded considerably since the old days. No, the old days were not that far behind me, but it was a world away. I felt broken, the feeling of which I could not at the time put into words. They had once called me a genius, "they" including pretty much everyone I knew. Not now: for if any had eyes to see, did any who had power of discernment could tell: now I was as seeming rather to be a stain left behind the former me's passing. Now, in the days since my mind had ruptured, and started bleeding dreams.

3 Not That Lucifer

All the weirdest things have happened to me when I was alone. Even 10/7/88, the most intense parts of that night happened while I was by myself (except, I will admit, the twisted satori—that sort of *required* someone else to have been there). It's as if having other people around is a sort of safety net; I can ground myself back into "reality" if I start floating off into my own thing. Being alone, I will also note, is a requirement to go on what is called the "Treasure Hunt." This was a literary device introduced to me in senior year of high school. There are 5 conditions. Those who (1) hunt for treasure (2) must go alone, (3) at night, and when they (4) find the treasure, they must leave some blood behind, and (5) the treasure is never what they expected. And of course I was searching for treasure. I was the White Pirate.

I got an apartment in Drexel Hill, PA, near my parents'. Completely alone, again. It was either that or start paying rent for staying at their place. No brainer to a man whose life was lived according to smoke. So, a mess of things happened to me when I lived there, the first of which was something the Lord Jesus Christ would say to me, I as being one who wanted the easy life, not so very different from everyone else. I, the devout atheist, casually thought about magic. Way before I considered myself a "paladin," I had thought to identify with the title, "warlock." And maybe the magic could save me from doing anything requiring effort? No, not like I believed in that sort of thing…

At one point, the Lord, the cartoon of whom I was looking at, embraced my head and said to me, "Work is magic." And all the signs snapped into place, implying then that a "work", one that was the result of great effort and craft, this was what magic I was really searching for. "Work" registered as 5 on the magic-o-meter that appeared in my imagination. No question about it, this was a lock. It wasn't until I dug out of the pit that simple 3 word sentence made any real sense. And after the Event that it had even deeper meaning. And *that* was magic in itself.

The other world was intruding a lot, and I was smoking pot like a chimney. Bought underneath the el train in Philadelphia's 63rd Street area, in the form of dime bags. It was in that apartment where I last dropped any acid, I think; weird: the trips were just intensification of the state I was already in. Yeah, be careful what you wish for, right? I had had a sticker on my old dorm room bed: "Quest for the eternal buzz". Well, there you go, ya idiot, ya dope. Late '92 through early '93 I was there in the Drexel Hill apartment, and working at that engineering company. And I was miserable. The pot sedated me enough, I suppose, to be functionally capable. Until came this one day.

I don't remember what the trigger was, but I just stopped participating in reality. I dropped out of life. I stopped going to work, stopped paying my rent, stopped paying my bills. Maybe it was something of clinical depression. It spoke of despair that nothing was going to get better. It was a form of giving up. Yeah, you know the consequences of these are not going to be wine and roses.

As I said, I was smoking a lot of pot at the time, and was being intruded upon by the other world, the visions, what I called the Halospace. So I don't remember much of the stuff that was happening, or perhaps in what order they may have happened. There was this one time when it was as if the top flew off of Halospace and something like psychic wind was blowing all around me, and I was led by angelic strand to fall down prostrate and to pray. I have no idea what I said, but after I spoke the prayer, I then took something of a measure of who had in the Halospace joined with my spirit in that prayer. I said, after "Amen," "All", meaning all the people of the cosmos had joined me. Only much, much later would the meaning of the "All Prayer" be revealed to me. That it had been an incursion of the War in Heaven when the top had blown off.

I remember learning about the secret, psychic life of trees, when they decided to talk to me through an Escher book. They said they speak to us, why books were made of paper, that they would be spirit guides for us. I remember naming a beautiful friend of mine (in the real world), the Great Spirit Gosh. (Where are you Billy Mitchell?) I wish I had kept in touch with him. And there was when the *actual* Great Spirit (Native American) took a look at my internals one day, sized me up, and named me, "crow-feather", and thus I was for many years from then on... Once, I could have sworn that marijuana resin appeared, as in, materialized at the edge of a razor blade I was using to scrape a book cover. I had been using that cover as a surface in general resin recovery from my smoking devices. (I would see better miracles later on.) The words from Jeremiah come to mind, Concerning the prophets: "My heart is broken within me; all my bones tremble. I am like a drunken man, like a man overcome by wine, because of the LORD and his holy words." [Jeremiah 23:9 NIV] Except that I *was* overcome with wine. Too.

I remember burning a dollar bill in an ashtray, George Washington's head turning black and in flames, then gone. And then I had a Bible I got from my high school English teacher, and was given the gift of this certain type of sight. It was like they were putting their point of view in place of mine, and I at this time could see the first page of Genesis from these points of view, of several personages through history: Vincent van Gogh, Albert Einstein, Leo da Vinci, and the strangest of all: Jesus Christ. Sure, the others were cool, but the Lord's was *something else.* It was like a desert wind—a holy, endless desert wind through the ink and paper. I didn't understand what that meant at the time, but I do now. This is indeed Son of the Infinite God. Literally. (You can use the present tense on him at any given time, ever.)

I wrote on the walls, I wrote in the books I had. (Mostly those books got lost somewhere along the way.) I remember the image of Mondrian's *Gray Tree,* and the rare Escher that I called the Doomsday Clock (which never rang). I have since scanned that image from the book where I had found it and it hangs on my wall. I remember Rosanna Arquette, and watching *The Big Blue* to see her move like poetry. And then there was this call: "Michael. Michael." Out of the expanse inside my mind. As if I were being called by the voice of God, back when I misinterpreted the passage in Revelation about the War in Heaven—for some reason, I was thinking Michael lost. I'm sure I was meant to read it the wrong way, of course. It was as if it were my fate to be doomed, a goner, to miss out on all the Good Stuff the saved would get in Heaven. I remember other people who called themselves Michael to take my place, brave souls. Myself, I hadn't yet found my courage. …and then I remember the notice slipped under my door: reality was going to evict me. Or at least, my landlord was. Any day now.

So, at one point I found that I was out of pot. And the car was out of gas (I can't say enough about that car: a Ford Escort stick my dad somehow made to have some kick in the engine, the vehicle that got me to work at the engineering company during my academic suspension, driving around smoking pot at night, and now, to go from the apartment to that workplace again—at least, before I stopped going completely: I had at some points driven it without glasses or contact lenses, I who can't see clearly past 4 inches without them; man, I loved that car). The night before, my friend Deniz had dropped by and gave me $20, which was all he had. Very nice of him. At that point in my life, he said that I was someone whose life had gotten out of control. I wouldn't have agreed, but really, what did I know? So, to go and pick up some pot, I was going to make the 3 mile trek on foot. And of course, it was raining. It became a somewhat epic adventure.

I went on a rant, speaking my internal dialog out loud to no one (well, the spirits in my head). Understand, though, I was making little if any sense at all. I stopped at a Wendy's and got just a small fries. I found a dime bag dealer at the usual place on 63rd Street, and then I knelt in the rain to pray. I could see our Lord and Mary Magdalene, and it was them versus us, me and Rosanna Arquette. What was I thinking, exactly? Heaven knows, because I certainly didn't. Don't try to make sense of it, would be my advice: but when I was prostrate on the city pavement in the rain, I felt like I was *invincible*.

As I got back, as I opened my apartment door, I made another one of those dramatic gestures, saying, "And it wasn't just a story. It was real!" Referring to *The Princess Bride,* a story about true love. At the time, I was applying it to me and Rosanna. Now, to understand what comes next, an aside: back before I had been drafted (10/7/88), earlier that year in the summer, I was completely in love with this girl. She lived in the Philadelphia area, so, it being the summer after her and my freshman year, I visited her every day. Her job was to drive those old-fashioned horse drawn carriages in Center City, giving a historical tour. I would park at 13th & South St. because that's as far east you can go before free parking ended, and then I would walk to 4th & Chestnut. It was a non-trivial walk, but I didn't think twice about it. Lovestoned, I think it's called now. By the end of the summer, my legs were all muscle and sinew (as one friend remarked at the time). So what does this have to do with anything? After the voyage in the rain to pick up my dime bag, my first long walk in some time, I was sitting in my main chair. I said, referring to that "arduous" walk and relating it to all that summer walking I had done for my previous infatuation, "Love. Really works the leg muscles." It made so much sense to me, just that little phrase. As I sat there, in the rest of the just, I thought it was the most profound thing ever.

But long story short, I guess of the story at this address, the landlord showed up a couple hours later with 2 police officers. There was still pot in the room, so I started acting *weird*. It worked, but how ironic: me pretending to be mentally divergent when it was the case that I could just mention talking to Albert Einstein, which I actually did. They bought it, but really, what was to buy? I was genuinely out there. They called for an ambulance to take me away, and they locked me up in the local loony bin. Would you believe it was all part of the plan? Not mine, of course…

About madness: that was the first time I'd been locked up for general weirdness. It was so long ago (1993) that they actually diagnosed me at the time with manic depression. (They call it bipolar nowadays. There's a song called "Manic Depression" that was on Jimi Hendrix's first album, so you have an idea that the term goes back.) I always thought that was wrong. The diagnosis, that is. Whether a certain mental illness itself is diagnosed wrong may be a non sequitur, though. Years later, when they got me on drugs that worked, they said the drugs were to treat paranoid schizophrenia. I was pretty happy with that. The diagnosis, of course. If I were happy with the schizophrenia itself I kept it to myself. Or even, from myself.

I have thought, when I was in the mood to consider such things, that I could have been diagnosed in the direction of schizo-affective disorder. But really, none of the diagnoses did justice to what I really did have, what was really going on with me. While it is true that there have been instances where I lost touch with reality, I have said so before: if you come right down to it, it is an acid trip that I never came down from. You could also mention that I was having visions from God, but they have something of a ground within the acid trip. There has always been a logic to my condition, if you look, that can be made sense of in terms of the world, the "sane" world. When asked by whomever, the very last time I was there, why I was in a funny farm, I told them what I just mentioned, "I have visions from God." It was the truth.

They say that you will know the difference between psychosis and a religious experience by what the effects are. If they mess up your life, it's the bad thing. If it heals you, then there's a better chance that it is God. Philip K. Dick and I—what to make of us? They seem in the middle, these experiences of ours, both damaging and healing, or maybe neither. Phil could carry on a normal life, but he was obsessed—till the day he died—because of the events of 2-3-74. He wrote *8,000 pages* about it. He wrote 4 novels about it. Was it God? Who can say? It didn't stop a suicide attempt, that's for sure. Though maybe they did stop him from dying from that attempt.

And me? The experiences, I must admit, have been intrusive at times. But they always end up helping me. I remember one Christmas card I got, from my brother, in which he wrote, "If you say that God is acting in your life, I believe you. Because you have turned your life completely around." But I get a bit far ahead of myself; that would come later. Right now I was still headlong down addiction's highway, and going into my first mental institution not because of what was going on in my head, but because I gave up. And as we descend, one must ask if one day we will face the heart of darkness? (You must go alone, at night…)

So the mythology going on in my head was, at the time—and it was a fluid thing—was that actually, the rebel angels had actually been the good guys, and the powers that be were the oppressors. I wasn't thinking that those powers were Jesus-based figures. I was working on my own Gnostic-type ideas. For instance, there was written in one Gnostic text that one of the Archons (one of the evil rulers of this material world) rebelled against Ialdabaoth, who was the god of this world, which was a fallen world. So I thought I was of that rebel's ilk in the rebellion, but not exactly. Don't ask me how it all worked out, I didn't have too much work go into its structure. Just a lot of nerve.

I called myself Lucifer Morningstar, the name I got not from the Bible, but the comic book *Sandman*, by Neil Gaiman. He added the "Morningstar", that is, since yes, the first half of the name does come from scripture. There was actually a competition I was in for this name, with Jim Morrison, who just kept it as "Lucifer". (He won that, by the way. Turns out it was not the type of thing you wanted to win.) If I was against God, it was because He was in the wrong, somehow: I had no intention of being evil. Though I really didn't think much on what made us fall, just how noble we were being rebels. Oh, and "we"? I thought my friends and such were the other "devils", like Asmodeus and Beelzebub. Like I said, it wasn't fleshed out to any significant depth. Good thing, too.

So at the initial hearing, the judge asked me, "What is your name?" to which I answered, "Lucifer Morningstar", and when he asked, "Where were you born?" I answered, "Heaven". And that was the end of the hearing, basically. With that kind of performance, they can lock you away. I think it was from a 3 day stay to become a 14 day stay. I found out being called "Lucifer" in real life does things to your head. It was just a phase, though. In and out the transom of desire.

I don't know what medication they put me on. I think it may have been Stelazine. I guess that helped me somewhat. It wouldn't be until 1997 that they would put me on the one that worked well on me, which was Zyprexa. It was new at the time, and expensive. My parents initially paid full price for it, another thing I owe them for. It still is expensive, even though there is a generic form, if you don't have the insurance to cover the costs. From 1997 on, the times I have had any sort of real trouble, mentally, was generally when I stopped taking meds. But it was as if each of those episodes ended in a way to get me back on those meds, as if that's built into the structure of such excursions. Strange, no?

I don't remember Philip K. Dick being on any kind of antipsychotic medication. I know Zyprexa certainly wasn't available to him at the time. And about him and me: why would you suppose that God picked a couple druggies to be his messengers, prophets for a new age? Maybe you could say ex-druggies. Phil wrote in *VALIS* that he had quit dope, and I for one haven't had anything stronger than cold and allergy medicine in over a decade. Well, those plus alcohol. And I know Phil still smoked a little pot, it was just that there was no more speed. But do drugs shape the mind a certain way that lends itself to religious type phenomena?

Is taking drugs something like knocking on the door to the unseen world? And God help you if anything or anyone answers, I might suppose. Perhaps some drugs are better than others to invite contact. But I look back on all his stuff: Philip K. Dick was truly a prophet. This is what a genuine prophet looks like as it is appropriate in this modern world. Neurotic, quixotic, brilliant, anti-establishment, troubled, frail but indomitable, colorful in speech and demeanor, a joker, a smoker, a midnight toker,[iv] just one of the good guys. You always knew what side he was on. You just thought he was kinda crazy.

In *VALIS*, PKD said, "The time you have waited for has come," and when I first read that, I thought what is natural to think about it—what Christians have thought starting the day that Jesus Christ left. I thought most probably what even Philip K. Dick himself thought: the end of the world is nigh! Yes, there was a reason why people think this, but is it ever correct? Yeah, no. The Lord himself (if not him, a direct line to him) conveyed to me that the Apocalypse doesn't happen for another 30, 40, or 50,000 years from now (counting from early 21st century). You who believed that the end time was near: what will it take to convince you otherwise? Is not the fact that St. Paul said that the Lord was coming back like tomorrow, when tomorrow was about 2000 years ago—how about that? How about the fact that the world has a nasty habit of not ending?

I, being the twin of a prophet, must be one myself, n'est-ce pas? So what is my message that I am inspired to give? For one, you could say I'm here to tell you that the time has come for all of us to grow up, for when I was a child, I spoke as a child, but when I grew up, I put away childish things. (Yes, paraphrasing St. Paul.) Because thinking that the end of the world is just around the corner brings about some very bad behavior. Irresponsibility like nothing else. People think great God will come from the sky, take away everything, and make everybody feel high. (And now to channel Bob Marley.) Get real. We might have needed that as spiritual milk, the thought that God was going to clean up our mess, but that idea is really getting long in the tooth. Time to start on the solid food, take responsibility for this place, our world, our home. Something is on the horizon, but it ain't the end.

Perhaps PKD understood something like this more than he realized. Back to the beginning, where Jesus Christ is the Lamb slain at the foundation of the world. By his perfect sacrifice, he brought down to us (or brought us up out of) the end of the Age of Iron (where the Black Iron Prison has its base), and thus the beginning of the Age of Gold. PKD called it the "Palm Tree Garden". I will call it the "Oasis". He thought that this was going to be brought about by a 5th messiah, and it would be Heaven on earth. Not quite. This prophet here, whose words you are now reading, is instead telling you that the Age of Gold is not Christ's return, but an earthly and natural phenomenon. Now, you may say, if the Lord's sacrifice was what brought the new age, where was this Oasis in the Dark Ages? You can't say that that was the Age of Gold! And I say, 1,000 years is as a day to God. And when the Lamb was slain, was he not 2 days in the earth, to rise on that 3rd day? So *now* is that time we have all waited for, according to we prophets 2: it is now to come to pass, the Age of Gold. Hearken: the Beginning is near.

4 Signs

Philip K., whose life is reflective of much prophecy, speaks of a woman who has died, and that all creation mourns after her. If you know anything about him, you would know that he had a twin sister who died in infancy, Jane. (Sonic Youth once named an album, *Sister* after Jane Dick, interestingly enough.) And you might know he wrote in *VALIS* of twin "hyperuniverses"—by which the universe was to have form and to have life—how one of them, the female, desired to be born before the right time, and so died, and this is how the creation of the world progressed. That was his explanation of why things are the way they are. There's a reason why the one I have is better. It's simple, really: he never tried to tie his back to the Bible. I will tell you why that is important, and why the Bible is holy—keep reading.

Phil then wrote that the healthy twin, the male, must be split in two to "repair" creation. Once again, to fit me into his myth(s), myself, I have one brother, who is very much alive, and Phil: Phil didn't seem to realize that he *was* one of the hyperuniverses (and of course, I was the other). Why we had visions. The job of splitting the "healthy twin" I saw being done, one pink and being Phil, one light blue and being me. But whether his myth has truth to it, as I said, we must somehow tie it to the Bible to be so. For that is the ubermyth that J. R. R. Tolkien talked about, (the idea of which so helped to convert C. S. Lewis to Christianity).

Yeah, it starts to sound crazy when you start to try and rewrite the beginning of the world in terms other than the Big Bang. Myself, I wrote a creation myth, too, a Gnostic one. But these days, I try and reconcile things that already exist. (Unless I happen to think of something unheard of.) Phil's myth is a modification of the Dogon story of creation. But he also talks about the

Gnostic Sophia, who seems at least tangentially related, who desired to know the Allfather before it was time, and inadvertently gave birth to Samael, the blind god—this was who was supposedly the actual creator of the material world. There is more to the story, but let us keep it relatively simple for now.

There is also the tale, from *Paradise Lost,* I believe, about how Lucifer had a daughter Sin, and copulated with her to give birth to Death. And of course, Sin and Death entered the world by way of Eve, who listened to the serpent over God, and spread these to Adam... and everyone else who would ever live. Sin, corresponding to being "born" in eternity, came into to being on Earth when Eve bit the fruit of knowledge of good and evil. If she had never sinned, Sin would never have been born, and so would not have had to die. Yes, it was Sin who was the woman who had died, the Devil's daughter, and there are reasons why all of creation laments this. But to see my mythology, between above and below, between eternity and now, there is a kind of feedback going on, in that.

I thought I was a Gnostic, back those decades ago. I think Phil did too. Unlike him, I had a lot of time to think about the stuff we both were thrown in the midst of. Maybe you think 8 years is a lot of time, but to grasp something that unfolds from infinity, it is less than a fraction. Looking from this point of view, that I have year upon year tried to improve upon, I cannot now hold with a lot of the ideas that Gnostics held to. The main one, which many were killed for, for heresy, was the idea that Jesus Christ, the actual spirit of him, was not truly human, and felt no pain when he was crucified. Or that the body was some guy, and the true Jesus Christ was a being of light, who did not undergo any crucifixion or death at all. These, I can't hold with.

What I have found is that whatever myths you want to make, it must fit somewhere in the context of the Bible. Perhaps not as exacting, cross-referenced fact, but whatever theory you come up with must make sense in Biblical terms. "Why?" you may ask. Well, it is not to satisfy some dogma. It is that for all that is wrong with it, it is only in the Bible that God says His name is "I AM". His name, just that. Not I am here, or I am there, or I am this, or I am that: none of the above: only, "I AM". It is to say that *I exist,* and I am the *only One* who exists as God. It is thus that the Bible is the Holy Bible. There is a story in Ezekiel where he was having a vision of the new temple, and the LORD passed through the east gate, so it was holy and never to be used. It is as such with this book. It is holy because it holds the Name of God.

It was written by human hands, however, not by angels on gold tablets, like the *Book of Mormon* was purported to have been. Well, except maybe the original 10 Commandments, which were purportedly written on stone by the hand of God Himself. But even those: there are 3 versions of them written in the Old Testament. Even that which was written by God Himself *on stone*—not even these, can everyone agree on. That tells you something about the Bible's "infallibility." I ask you, who is greater, the one who makes no mistakes and is always perfect, or the one who can take something imperfect and make it perfect? For to know that the Book would have errors in it, but to make of those imperfections even better than if it were all perfectly transcribed from the mouth of the Lord down into ink: this is *my* God, and my God is greater than the naïve idealization derived from the shallowest of that book's readings. To hold the Bible so high, above the love of people: remember that the Sabbath was made for man, not man for the Sabbath:[v] do not make the scriptures another idol to be worshipped. It is true that for all of us it acts as the last stand on any question of faith, but it is not the beginning and the end in and of itself. It is not God, even if we can say it is truly God's word.

For one thing, it is wrong about Judas, at a couple points. From what I have seen, is not wrong when it says that it is Judas who hands over Our Lord to the authorities. (And it is important that this distinction is made: it is "hand over", not "betray".) But where it says he is the son of perdition, it is incorrect. There has been scholarship done to this effect, some bold enough to proclaim that you should not be surprised when you see Judas seated ahead of you in Heaven. And for my part, Judas was one of the spirits I met in my visions, though pretty late in the game did I identify him as one of the good guys.

So we get to the pudding, where the proof is supposed to be: what happens when the Bible says, or you think it says, something that you can't get behind? Chew on that question a second. One might think of the words of Isaac Asimov, when he said, "Never let your sense of morals get in the way of doing what's right." Get it? Right? I know that even if you do get that, this doesn't mean that I'm expecting you to just turn around and think of Judas in a completely different light. But this attitude also means that *I* cannot look at the question of Judas in the same light I did before, after I got to know Judas in my visions, saw what he was about. Let us say that I as a jury of one cannot convict Judas Iscariot of the conspiracy to murder Jesus Christ beyond a reasonable doubt. He was fulfilling a purpose when he did as he did, a purpose given to him by Jesus Christ himself. And there is even a purpose to why his name has been dragged around in the dirt lo these two millennia. Remember, to follow dogma when it goes against your heart is one of the faces of death. [See Appendix: Judas Iscariot]

And death? Myself, I don't think I ever feared death enough. Right after my mind exploded, I thought that committing suicide would be a convenient way for me to join the spirits I had been talking to. Any true suicidal thoughts would fall by the wayside, by and by, but these weren't thinking that it was the end of life, merely passing from one world into another. I tried like 20 Tylenols, and that just made me sick the next morning. We had tomatoes growing in the backyard, so I ate a bunch of their leaves, which I read were poisonous. Nothing. I wondered then if that claim of toxicity were a correct account. Then I swallowed a bunch of Stelazine, and that made want to crawl out of my skin, but they didn't kill me. Stupid reality was hard to get rid of.

I did once put a loaded rifle up to my chest and touched the trigger. My father had a few rifles *and ammunition* in the bedroom closets at the house. I don't know what was more stupid, doing the little playing chicken with myself and an M-1 or leaving it around for me to play with, in the condition I was in. But there, one might say, it may be revealing that really it wasn't that I wanted to die: I wanted to escape. And the landscape in my head was the fantasy I wanted to escape to. At least, it was the closest.

Well after being released from the mental place, after being evicted from the apartment, I was allowed to visit my brother in Berkeley, California. I was not in good shape, if I think back on that time. I remember having my first hit of pot after a couple three months of deprivation: I simply declared, "I feel normal." High had become my normal state of being, and down was unnatural to me. Which is sort of a sad thing, if it ever happens to you. But there you go, welcome to the monkey house.[vi] I putzed around trying to make what little cash I had stretch to buy me food along with those drugs. And then this happened: before I was to return to my parents' house, the cartoon image of the Lord Jesus Christ shut my visions down. Maybe it was not a comprehensive cure, but for the most part, my imagination became—if not completely the same as—similar to a normal mind. For the next stretch of time, I was alone when I was alone. Here and there were minor incursions from the Halospace, but I was for the most part, strangely normal. But the normal wasn't my old self: I still wasn't a genius anymore. Indeed, I was damaged goods.

I was living with my parents, living a failure's life. Sorry if I offend anyone, if maybe you have that kind of life—especially if that is what you have fought for—but I had been the vaunted golden child, with such possibility before the drugs had gotten to me. Now, I got a job as a lowly administrative assistant, a job which I hated. The Lord visited once, peripherally, and asked what was it I really wanted. I couldn't think of anything, not really. I didn't know. He said then that it looked like I was lost. I was getting pot with every spare dollar, and that wasn't easy, as my parents were closely monitoring my income and purchases. I had to get receipts for everything, and they all had to add up. Dad enrolled me in a rehab program, which I drove to once a week. I remember going there once while I was high. And the counselor wasn't able to tell. After a while, they said I was done. Cured. My dad was quite surprised when I told him that, because he could definitely tell I wasn't clean and sober. The thumbs up was the result of me heaping upon them a pile of lies, fabricating a full (enough) life I wasn't leading. Yes, I was still a liar.

I got fed up again with this kind of life, like I had when I was living in the apartment in Drexel Hill. So one payday, I got my check, promptly cashed it, then I basically stole my parents' minivan, driving to 63rd street where I bought some pot, and then went to a massage parlor (yup, that kind of massage parlor). I lived out of the minivan for a few days, visiting the few friends I still had in the area whenever I could. After the money was gone, I checked into the mental hospital I had stayed in before, telling them that I was having suicidal thoughts. Which meant they basically couldn't refuse me entrance. I had a health insurance card, so that was covered. A successful escape.

I called my parents, and they were furious. During my stay they gave me lots of drugs, none of which seemed to give me any sort of high whatsoever. When I was being released, I was *that* close to ending up at a homeless shelter. But no, my parents took me back, God bless them. Now, however, *they* were fed up. They were going to exile me, I guess you could say, to a place in the middle of nowhere, in Korea—at a farm. A Christian farm, run by a famous pastor. That's what the dice popped up, anyway, when I had rolled the bones this time around.

For the most part, not much happened on the farm. Nothing supernatural, you might say. I was there only for a few months. I lost weight from not eating meat all the time, and I got a deep tan from working outside. The schedule was, wake up for morning prayer, breakfast, work from 8am to noon, lunch, break until 2pm, work from 2pm to 6pm, dinner, evening prayer, and then just collapse at around 10pm from being so wiped out. My favorite job was digging, and I don't know why that was. I didn't like working with the chickens, for some reason. I was a mystery to myself, as yet. I didn't take any meds, I didn't do any drugs besides maybe nicotine (I was a smoker, back when, for about 17 years). And like I said, mostly the other world did not intrude. But you could say one important thing did happen, there on that farm.

In the midst of the summer heat, fortune brought with it some visitors to the farm. As mentioned, the pastor who ran it was famous, at least in some circles, and enough outside people knew about it that they took a group of kids in for a couple weeks, a sort of summer program to learn all about service to God or some such thing.

It was a mostly suburban crowd, mostly kids; but there was a guy there that was around my age, who was one of the leaders of the trip. So, once the kids realized that I was not one of the natives (because my skin was so tan they initially thought I was a permanent resident), I was arguing with the kids about the (non)existence of God, with me having been a devout atheist from about age 18 on. And they were kids, right? They didn't know anything, so I clobbered them with my pseudo-intellect. At that point they introduced me to that guy, the one who stood as of the leaders, and as I talked to him, he basically started to cut right through my bull patties, and told me how he came to be saved, and we talked about Jesus Christ... and all the signs were just right, all the signs that made anything make sense to me. We went outside to the path that led in through the forest, and we prayed. That was where I became a Christian, for real. Nothing supernatural at all... except maybe my reading of signs.

    I don't remember when exactly I started basing my decisions on signs. I seem to recall before my mind exploded that I usually did not think in words, but rather as a smooth, if not fluid semantics, punctuated by flashes of insight or observation. It was what might be considered pure thought. I would learn, along the way on with this story, how to think in words, and why one should try to do this. I once examined the result of two observations I had while in pure thought mode, and I tried to put them into words. One of them was wrong. What it forces you to do is to check their logic, because the stream model is more of a guess how things flow from one to another, and it is prone to misconnections. It's like judging a book by its cover, and what feels like the correct progression may only just look like one.

    Before learning the ways of clear logic, and when my psyche cracked, logical thought seemed to be replaced by reading signs, like the numbers having meaning, or some coincidence pointing to a prediction or conclusion. This is what happens when you really let yourself go, mentally. And get perhaps more broken than I might have thought. Reading signs, however, got me in trouble at times. Because like a lot of those who read signs, one might believe it is God sending secret messages to you. The phenomenon usually may be observed as—thinking about how we perceive things at all—your brain seeing a pattern you think is related to the patterns that govern the world, or how it works. But it is like the casing of an insight without the sausage filling it: having no vigorous test to see if it is indeed correct in thinking so, and maybe even that that trick of the mind's eye is mistaking art for science. Not that art has no place among us, and sometimes it can pull off a scientific thing or two, but that's not what it's for. You can draw a pretty graph, but without the equations to back it up, the best you can have is a definite maybe.

Anyway, after the conversion, I wasn't a *practicing* Christian for years. I went through the periods of being the annoying Christian, which some never grow out of—like since you don't partake of a certain bad thing anymore, that now everyone else who currently do partake are suddenly "sinners," while you're the saint. Maybe 4 years after the path in the forest was the first time I went to church without anyone having sent me there. By then I was thousands of miles and another world away.

The visions eventually returned to me, after I had escaped the farm (or they let me leave) and my aunt and I visited Thailand. Where, of course, I got my hands on a little pot, in an excursion from the hotel room we were sharing, as soon as she fell asleep. That definitely did something, because while I was reading *Atlas Shrugged,* there they were again: Jesus, Einstein, Rosanna Arquette, Joan of Arc, et al. I felt at times I was greater than Christ, and at other times, that I was damned as the Antichrist. I blame the latter on one small slip. And too, I thought a lot that I was the Archangel Michael. This was another thing exceedingly useful.

It seemed like an organic process, starting from the call of "Michael. Michael." in the apartment. I was starting to gain some courage, and I'm not sure exactly where that came from. Mysterious forces always seemed to be working in my life, and have I ever seemed aware at merely the barest surfaces of them. Somewhere along the line, I stopped thinking Michael lost the War in Heaven. And to be him—it seemed like it were a given thing that that was what I was, something I would naturally fulfill, to step into such well worn shoes… especially this one time I contended for the pillars of creation. (There are 4.)

    I was just getting out of bed at my aunt's house in Seoul, after the visions had returned. And the experience of something unleashed in Heaven just struck me in the face. Beyond the cloud of unknowing there was a sudden clarity: these four lines cut through the fabric of imagination, just *going,* and it was as if whispered to me (perhaps by Gabriel?) that these were the underpinnings of existence itself. There was as if a sizzling sound released by those lines, following them through the ether of the imagination, but in an expanded version, where it was sort of in the air before me—in the Halospace, where vision meets mind. Then was there an evil force threatening to bend the lines into malevolent design. I held on with my own will, as the will of the heart may press on, to bring them back into a benign path. But what was I to do? Was it merely to hold on?

    At just that point, in the Halospace was a cartoon of a seated, faceless man who said something like, "When contending for the ground of creation, stay to the soft things, for even the hard things rely on the soft." And the other side returned that soft things are good to terrorize and eat by the hard things… and it was thus in which they lost. I put my finger on my sternum, concentrating on the softness of the skin between my finger and the bone under it. And the lines flew off, away and away, and I began to feel safe once more.

At that point, I was jubilant. Or more precisely, (also) manic. I stormed out of my aunt's house, and had a running dialog going with the Lord before all the beings of creation as I marched through the streets of Seoul, which went so:

"Archangel Michael, what did you do?"

"Annihilated the universe!"

"With what?"

"Nothing!"

"Is this nothing?" the Lord pointed to a patch of black.

"Yes!"

And then I signed off by showing myself, a somewhat golden yellow globe, kind of winking at Rosanna Arquette. I held myself aloft just for a second, and then I was gone from my own vision into the Halospace. One might conceive such views as like looking at yourself in a dream. Now, done with my report, I went back to my aunt's place. I calmed down. Only after the War was over did I learn that the actual Archangel had been there with me in that report, and was so incoherent while feeling so great himself because he had *just come* from casting Satan from Heaven!

5 Work Is Magic

Are we, are we, are we ourselves? Are we ourselves and do we really know?[vii] I remember looking at myself in the mirrors when oft I was on acid, and thinking, this is not really me. Even after I stopped my LSD intake I would think, "Who are you?" when looking at my reflection. And there were times along the way I know I wished I could be someone else, some*thing* else. And so, ask and it shall be given you? I would be granted this wish, when I believed myself to be the greatest of the angels. Michael, not Lucifer—Luc pissed his greatness away. The Archangel, however, was not the only identity I ever assumed.

There was once when I was talking to the angels in Halospace, and thinking much of myself, said something I would come to regret for years to come: "I was supposed to be the Antichrist? Scary." Implying my so called power was so great as to have been potentially an overwhelmingly big problem to the good guys. Pride. My only enemy. So the angels said to me, "But that means, YOU LOSE." And that kicked out the pedestal I was standing on. (I had defined winning as going to Heaven, losing going to Hell.) I think what had been previous to this bubble burst was me comparing myself to the Lord, and me thinking I was better than him because I had marked out a higher position than him on some arbitrary measure. Ignoring that he was represented by an intricate golden globe and me, I was a black triangle. (The globe, BTW, I found out was the *actual* Morning Star.)

The truth of the matter was, of course, that I was never either the Archangel nor the Antichrist, but those two delusions served as useful crutches through the years I was in the pit. Through the madness. The madness that saved me. In striving for a glory that I apparently had lost along the way, but I would work to regain. Or in the terror in thinking I was damned, which served as some good negative reinforcement, but was the unpleasant stick, in the carrot and stick model. Count it all joy, however.

Now it was, in my aunt's place, that on the cusp of sleep, when I came up with *such* an idea. At the time, I didn't even put it into words—that would come later. The idea was delineated in protowords, like semantics from which could form the words I was thinking of: the Tree of the Forgetting of the Knowledge of Good and Evil. (It's a much smaller mouthful when described in protolanguage.) In other words, a return to the primeval innocence, no matter what one has suffered through in life. I think in Heaven it exists, but before my thought of it, I have never heard tell of such a possibility. To this day I think it's one of the best things I've ever thought of, or in fact, one of the best things *anyone* has ever thought of. One of those things that you don't even need to write down, so powerful is the thought. That was one of the high points in that local nadir of my existence.

About this time, I could be identified by a certain Korean word, pronounced "chengpyon"—it means "a disgrace". That was what I was, a failure. I sat around my aunt's living room in Seoul, talking to the cartoons floating around in my mind's eye, which were spilled into the visual field of reality, as like a palimpsest, a transparent layer overlaid upon the material world. I really can't remember much in the way of the things that I would think about, what the cartoons would say to me. I was like a turtle in a cage, wandering only in the small space allotted it. I seem to remember thinking that I was the Antichrist, off and on, and learning how to pray. I guess perhaps I was getting better, after all. It was just not all fireworks, I suppose.

They were giving me some powder medicine which did nothing but taste bad going down. I felt like those Bob Marley lyrics: "Is there a place for the hopeless sinner / Who has hurt all mankind just to save his own beliefs?" Rather, I felt like I was living those lyrics. I was like I were being persecuted from within myself. And then to think, thinking back, that this was not the bottom. There were tiers down from there to go before I would comprehend what I was meant to know. One thing I learned in the path I went down was that there is *always* a worse that things can get.

I was tasked to read the Bible, at times, and besides TV, it was the only thing from outside myself that was allowed in. Or at least it seemed that way, since I don't speak Korean—it might have just been an interpretation of the circumstances. Do you believe in the Bible? The spectrum of belief goes from something like the fundamentalist, who claims to take the entirety of it literally, at face value (who seem always to stumble on the command, "Love your enemies"). And it ends at the other side with an atheistic appreciation of fictions written by human beings which at best turns people docile, at worst into killers, with a special gleam in their eyes. In this first reading of it, however, I wouldn't turn out to be anything based on the writings therein. The words went right through me. Or over my head.

It is true, however much the fundamentalist would have us believe, that we cannot think the writers of scripture meant for the text to be taken as error-free history. That was never their intention. It is, in fact, a sort of blasphemy, a human being telling God exactly what He was supposed to have said. What it is, at the foundation: a means of looking at ourselves and the world as if there is a greater purpose for all things. That's it. In it are things that are true, as is so with the other great religious writings from around the world. It is what things *are* true when we compare it to other sacred texts which serve to differentiate it. There are things that are true in other texts which do not appear in the Bible, but as we have established, in the Bible is the Name of God. Hard to compete with that.

Early Christians didn't have a Bible, outside of the Old Testament. There were only two tenets of the faith: do you believe in Jesus Christ, resurrected; and, have you received the Holy Spirit? And perhaps to see about getting baptized. Might these, then, be the specific things that are to be held true of the faith today? And it would seem to me that now that we have a Bible (a "full" Bible, of both Old and New Testaments), we overlook the second condition and only count the first.

Have you received the Holy Spirit? What would be the sign of that? Does it even have relevance anymore? No one looks for spirits anymore, in general practice. We have school spirit, the spirits of the dearly departed in their old photographs, but no real "spirits". In the New Testament, it says that you would know Christians as ones impervious to the effects of poison; and able to handle snakes; and also, with the ability to heal disease by the laying on of hands. There are people even now who take that inventory literally. (Have you not heard of the snake handlers?) I would call such predilections putting new wine into old wineskins. But in modernizing the question, do we dilute it? How about this: you have received, yea verily, the Holy Spirit when you have learned to love one another with all your heart, and stand by that love, stand up for that love? This would be the new wineskin.

One observes, instead, that people tend not to want to receive the Spirit of Love: they want to close themselves up, whether solo or with a group that shares their prejudices. Such crowds are the worst, who with hive mind can conduct ignorance and hate like waves upon the water. They'd certainly rather not open up, especially to new ideas, or strange people. They want to take care of their own, and the rest of the world be damned.

And anyone that doesn't believe in the things they believe? They are the "others," and those "others" are certainly children of the Devil, and don't deserve the rights of the true believers, like us. We have our own truth. We would surely not have killed the prophets. We would surely not have crucified Christ. Jesus Christ was a white man. Jesus Christ was an American! ... Yeah. When someone or some mass of people cannot be reached, except in terms of a false reality, to refute them is to become contaminated by their unreality.[viii] At that point, it seems like the only thing you can do is shake the dust from your sandals and move on.

It is that some of us just can't realize how wrong we are. We don't see our own blindness by the fact of our blindness, a terrible feedback loop. The difference between good and evil, then, is that when shown the error of one's ways, the good, the human shall repent. He will be sorry and do his best not to do it again. This is repention. (Knowing that how worse the wrongdoing, the harder it would be to acknowledge that wrong.) The evil, the inhuman will not be sorry. They will try and make it seem like what they did was right. Whatever needs to be twisted around to his point of view, the inhuman thinks not twice of attempting that twist. This is what it means to be unrepentant. Knowing these two sides, for good reason is it thus, that the sacrament of confession teaches us to own up to our wrongs.

We then touch upon the War in Heaven again. Unlike the evil human, the evil angels were privileged to be within an environment where so much more could be conceived than down here, resembling a state where anything was possible. What the good angels fought against was right turning into wrong, wrong seeming as right, and to remove the evil angels from the root controls of all existence.

I wouldn't know that for lo, the years to come—there, then, sitting in my aunt's living room, in Seoul, talking to the people in my head. Everyone had sort of given up on me at that corner in my life. And there was also this: I have thought that in my madness that I committed atrocities for no reason, crimes against humanity as a sick joke. I didn't even laugh. I have thought that if I make it to saint, that I would love the Lord more than any other: for he would have forgiven more in me than them, even murderers were not guilty of having destroyed the souls of their victims, which I have imagined I have done. How different is it than a commander ordering the death of innocents he never sees in person? And if the Lord will not count those against me, he cannot count in my favor my imagined heroics. I was saved, ultimately, from myself. Before I did something excessively stupid to myself.

And sitting in my aunt's living room, talking to the people in my mind, I was a tumbler with three positions: someone who was the leader in the work for the salvation of all the world, for I was not fully a believer in the Lord Jesus Christ, and so saw myself as competition to him; the Archangel Michael, fighting the good fight, whatever tasks came in the ether, loyal to Jesus Christ to the last; and the Antichrist, the sudden and burning fear which made me go to my knees, and pray for mercy. Those little fear episodes never lasted too long, though. The Lord would always show me mercy when I prayed for help. All of it ending up, figuring down and down the line, that I was none of these.

Of course, I hadn't hit rock bottom yet. But speak of the devil. For some reason, the Rosanna Arquette cartoon person was upset with me. It might possibly have been because I was not the kind of man she wanted, what she expected a savior to be, so she let out her anger over that situation by emasculating me. (The floggings will continue until morale improves. That kind of logic.) She was a little confused, and I probably had a hand in how she got that way. But now, she would pretty much strip me of any pride, whatsoever. She humiliated me, then blamed me for getting humiliated. She would try with all her might to defeat me at tests of will, and then she would tell me she had wanted to be defeated. I will describe the worst of what she did to me in a second. Her actions upon my waking hours caused my aunt to go and lock me up. I would strain against Arquette until I would shake. So my aunt put me away, not at a hospital, but at an involuntary rehab center, mostly alcoholics. Prison-ish. Now there really were bars on the windows.

The persecution didn't end at that point. Perish the thought. It was there that Arquette would perform her *opus magnum*: she started doing a little thing, where she would stop me from pissing. Oh, it doesn't sound like much because you probably take it for granted, like I used to. But to have such a fundamentally normal thing disrupted is seriously a form of torture. And I don't think she ever got how bad it was for me.

I'd stand there, ready to go, when she yanked on some sort of line connected psychologically to my junk, and so I would strain, and strain, and strain... nothing. Dejected, I put it away, and as I turned to walk out, no, no, no: she would yank a second string, which made me want to go again, and repeat. One night, I started to try at 10pm, and after try, after try, after try, I finally let out a stream at 4am. But all this time, it was that I didn't realize I was learning something very important. (And it was not Arquette's intention for me to learn this. She was just being evil.) This served as a penance for my ruining of my life with drugs, as one who had had *such potential*. Where's your messiah now?

Also going on in the rehab place was there was this 19 year old tank of a young man who had it in for me. And I at that time was still a coward, and I did nothing to stand up for myself. This was also another hard lesson learned: do not provoke something with the capability of belligerence if all you have in your corner is a philosophical policy on non-violence. He bullied me for a few months, and if you've ever been bullied you know that that feels more like being terrorized. Not quite this bad, though: my God, my God, why have you forsaken me? It can always be worse. And, you know, that little rough patch of road… I got through it. It seemed, later, like all a part of the Plan.

After the experience of such unmitigated, systemic *failure* on my part (and note that it wasn't the end of the failure, but the point comes naturally here), the words the Lord had said to me, back at the Drexel Hill apartment a couple years previous, they got a new, profound meaning: "Work is magic." I got an idea of the cosmos like no one else because of those words, and the meaning to them that I'd earned.

When you drop something, you expect it to fall. You've tried this, correct? Never do you doubt that when you drop anything else, too, it will also fall. No one in history, as far as we know (those who never went up into outer space or some such thing) has ever had it that gravity failed to pull down that ball, that bone, that rock, after you drop it. It's one of the sure things about this universe, this being like some of your basic forms of logic: logic was itself possible because of things being sure. These things *just work*. To question their functioning is preposterous; incorrect to the highest and lower tiers of reasoning; the idea of them not working is just something we never think about, really. Do you see where I'm going with this? Will you stop and wonder why you never wondered why?[ix]

See, that's the thing when all you ever try fails 19 times out of 20. Even down to the most basic of human functions, to piss! To anyone without prostate cancer or something else horrible: this is supposed to work! *Just work!* Do you see it yet, where I'm going with this line of thinking? What if the necessary is not necessary? Imagine that gravity is not a sure thing just because we have equations saying that it should be so. This is of the nature of David Hume's Problem of Induction. What if logic itself did not necessarily hold to be true, or consistent? What if things like truth were specifically made that way, on purpose? That was in the War in Heaven: the opponents wanted something more malleable than was "allowed" by how things worked, in any way that made sense. To kill the Logos. This sort of thinking, I found out, makes a Hell out of Heaven. And if a single angel had lost to his evil opponent, that would have been the end of the world as we know it, to awake instead to something ultimately utterly incomprehensible.

So first, because of the scope and efforts of the winning of the War, we should thus not take the most basic aspects of the universe for granted. Second, we should understand that we were not ever guaranteed that things should work at all: the world was made by design so that any functioning was and is possible in it. So third: this was what I learned as a deeper meaning of "Work is magic": to someone who has had everything fail on him, when in those rare instances, something—anything—works, it *is magic*. And it turns out, *this is the correct way to look at the world*.

We don't notice that miracles happen every day simply because they happen every day. Taken from the point of view that the most basic things we take for granted are not somehow guaranteed to have been as they are, to work, we need to see how incredible is our debt to creation—and if there is a creator, to that entity. And I do comprehend the mystical view that the cosmos basically created itself, but this does not erase how much a blessing the world and things of the world are. I know what name(s) I call my own idea of the Creator, but even if yours has a different face, or different idea of being, if that One is as responsible for all things as mine is, you will find the number of your blessings uncountable. As will be the gratitude that you and I owe.

I think it does take something to make you aware of how incredible the gift of everything is. For the fish has no idea what water is. And to see how intricate is destiny: at some points a hairsbreadth away from the ruin of it all, or even where an incredible event that could end up changing not just yourself, but the world—*not* to have such an event happen, when all the signs point to its coming. The music of fate includes the absence of things as well as the inclusions. And to think what a miracle it is, a second chance. I keep thinking I'm on my fourth.

After getting out of rehab, I putzed around a little, but then decided to go back to school. This was my second chance progressing in force. The policy on returning from leave had changed from 5 years to 4, but I grandfathered in. Good thing I could just return from the leave of absence, because I would have had to reapply otherwise, and with my grades that would have been a tough sell. Then, when I was there, I had to find an old professor in a class I'd practically never attended to get an "incomplete" grade updated to a "D". It was pure luck that I located him on campus and that he remembered me. After all, 5 years is a considerable space to bridge on such scant traces.

I lived in an apartment off campus, and my aunt lived with me, keeping my nose clean to any degree she could. I got high at every opportunity, though. I was more the Archangel Michael (having a human form) than anyone else during those days, and you know, it was like in the movie *Kingdom of Heaven:* when Balian is asked, "Does making a man a knight make him a better fighter?" he replies, "Yes." Thinking I was something great (just down on his luck) made me aim higher. That semester I returned I got 3 A's and 1 B: that's Dean's List, baby!

I would go and do something stupid, though. That Thanksgiving vacation, I got into some sort of argument with someone in my head, probably Arquette. Don't ask how, but I ended up signing over my soul to the Devil, in exchange for *nothing*. I don't remember if I signed it in blood or not. I think I might not have gone that far, though I am suspicious that my memory simply does not record such stupidity. That wasn't beneath me, in other words.

At some point later, a cartoon that was unmistakably the Lord sort of pulls me aside and says to me, "Wh-y-y did you do that?" Sort of an inscrutable smile on his face. I mumbled something whereupon he declares, "Oh, you didn't *mean* it?!?" And I see a picture of a blob which is my soul, and he releases a couple wires or hooks or something that had latched on me. To the story of selling one's soul to the Devil for recompense, he called it "a myth"—in other words, no one ever in history got something for signing over his soul. Not literally, at least.

The consequence for that stupidity: I no longer thought I was St. Michael. You might think that would be a blessing, but like I have written, that was rather a benign delusion. And now, this was just before the movie *Michael* came out. I would be St. Michael again sometime later, before I would be free from that delusion forever, but the glee that would have come in thinking oneself being depicted on the silver screen, I would never experience.

And then came next semester. It was supposed to be my last. I was taking 6 classes, if I remember right—overload, all I needed to graduate. And my aunt was not there anymore, I was on my own; and that ended up being a bad thing. Of course, I would get some pot every chance I could get, and now I could smoke it at home with impunity. Even though I had few funds, I found ways to procure said weed. Once a dealer gave me a full ¼ ounce for $5 because he heard about my monetary situation and felt sorry for me. And there was also that at one point I'm pretty sure I stopped taking my Stelazine. I was therefore starting to get zoney, you know, spacing out at homework sessions; I was starting to miss assignments; I couldn't cope with dealing with two worlds at a time, so I ended up dropping out of one of them again. I did the right administrative things in doing that, thank the Lord: I dropped all my classes and emailed all the groups I was associated with, and got a partial refund on tuition *(very* partial, $2,500 out of $7,500). Dad would be furious about it all, of course.

So what did I do then, while drifting in between worlds again? I hung out in campus dorm lobbies watching music videos, continuing to get high whenever I could (though my wallet was no help now, blanked without anything to fill it in), and I was talking to St. Michael, St. Gabriel, Jesus Christ, and Rosanna Arquette in my head. Many crushing and sizzling rushes of fear, now that I was starting to fail again, and in salvation's doghouse—believing I was damned as the Antichrist, over and over, being let off the hook after each time, though. It was my 27th year of existence, the year Jimi Hendrix, Jim Morrison, etc., etc. all died in. Maybe I was lucky to survive it. Harsh times, but you know? I'd had worse.

I remember walking around, out in the Pittsburgh winter. With my eyes half in the Halospace. I once walked from CMU to the end of downtown Pittsburgh, and then back again. I saw on a couple of walks the *real* Beast 666, straight up, but maybe depowered some—I probably wouldn't have handled the encounter well without the forces of evil watered down, as it were. And everyone was mad at me again; I was failing again, flopping around and accomplishing nothing—nothing real. But this time would be the last: I was finally, here, beginning to repent of my sins. Turning over a new leaf. With prejudice.

My parents visited, and needless to say, they were not happy. They were not immediately prepared to take me back, though, and they left me in Pittsburgh for a little while longer. Then they sent my aunt again, to take care of me as she would, again. I then did end up at another mental place, in Pittsburgh. It was quite nice. And there I had a pivotal moment. I asked this guy, another patient, "So, why are you here?" To which he replied, "Oh, I have visions of the Virgin Mary. She looks like my girlfriend and is standing on a vagina, but I know it's her." Yeah. I thought, "Dude, *you're nuts!*" ...which made me realize, "That's how *I* sound to *other people!*" It was a stunning realization.

Rosanna Arquette left me when I was staying at that mental hospital. I guess she couldn't take the failure anymore. Years of it, pretty much all she knew about me. And then once they released me, my parents came and got me again. Back to the old house, where I grew up. They gave me a choice: work at the hardware store (my father's) all day, or wake up for 6am mass every day, but the day would me mine. So, 6am mass it was. But it was not like the other times. For the first time, my parents were not the enemy, and I was honest about what I'd done. I repented.

As this chapter ends, the angels and the Lord had started laughing at me, right after Arquette had left. But armed with my stunning realization with the Virgin Mary guy, I thought the forceful thought over all of it, "You're just a psychosis trying to keep me down!" And the laughter stopped. The images sort of faded: not completely, but it was a new day. I had stopped believing in it.

I would—for years after—describe my "condition" as, "I took an acid trip in 1991 that I didn't come down from until 1997." Which is impressive enough. But there would be so much more. There would be a reason for it all.

6 Recovery

So, it wasn't real, it was nothing. It was an accident of fate. I never talked to any of those people, and hey, some of those people were *alive,* anyway. Maybe you could have talked to ghosts of the dead, and the angels, and Jesus, but Rosanna Arquette's *alive, dude,* and she has no idea who you are in real life. Yeah, it was quite a dream, though… (And then in the movie the protagonist finds some charm that came back with him from the dream world. This is not a movie, though. It's too *weird* to be a movie.) At least, did you leave some blood behind? Did you find what you were looking for? Did you at least figure out what it *was* that you were looking for?

I was just crazy, right? They have medication for what I have. Yeah, they did not fail to classify and categorize me, after all. Not so unique as all that. I would fly under this banner for 15+ years. Ex-psycho. Ex-druggie. Though I wouldn't completely quit pot for a few years in this next phase, and the "trip" I supposedly came down from in '97 never completely left me. No, I never completely came down. It was always sort of there, backstage, lurking. And every once in a while, I would let down my guard, and BLOTTO!

I found, much later of course, something that would be relevant for all these years lost in Halospace. I quote the late great Harry Potter here. He asks Dumbledore, "Is this real? Or has this been happening inside my head?"

To which Dumbledore replies, "Of course it is happening inside your head, Harry, but why on earth should that mean that it is not real?"[x]

Do you see how that makes sense to me? It does in ways you cannot imagine. Or maybe you can. Though, you know, there would be quiet times, too, as far as the visions go. Now, after they took me home from school, my parents and I really talked. I was honest with them for the first time in years and years. Maybe ever. I didn't know, however, if they would ever understand all of what really happened to me. But right then, I finally began to honor the 5th commandment: "Honor thy father and thy mother, so that thy years may be long upon this world." Something like that, right? Yeah, I still wanted to smoke pot, but now I felt bad about doing it. At least I had quit acid. And eventually, the marijuana would fall by the wayside, too, but even now, I have faint memories of what the sensation of those feel like. If there is a genetic memory, it's been wired in there.

I went back to school in the summer, to take 2 classes, and my (younger) brother was looking after me. He let me smoke weed, but I didn't go crazy on the stuff. I got A's in both of the classes. Not that much happening that summer. Then my aunt was back with me for fall semester '97, my last one. And I did it. I graduated. Not with honors, of course, just one Dean's List, but understand that a lot of my early college buddies got sidetracked and either didn't graduate or not from CMU. I was officially a Bachelor of Science in Mathematics and Computer Science. It was not that hard.

I did have to take a senior level math class after a 5 year break from anything like adding 2 numbers together, but (Lord be praised) I found help, a math major named Brian. (I tried to find him, years later, to properly thank him, but he as yet even now has eluded my search.) I found out, actually discovered this after the first semester back: if you go to class, and you do the homework, *you'll do well.* It had just never occurred to me before. What an idiot (me).

The year after I graduated was quite different than the Drexel Hill apartment. It wasn't a stopgap period where I was working as an interim assignment. This was it, a start in the real world, to land on my two feet for the first time ever, really. It did take till September of '98 to find a job, at a startup in San Francisco named XUMA, in the city I'd moved to. That was right after I took a night class at Berkeley, filling a gap in my skills. I started well below your normal starting salary, but man, I was happy to find a job in the field I had studied for.

It must be told, actually though, that I had had this idea about becoming a writer and writing novels in my spare time. But the Zyprexa made me antsy: I couldn't sit for 8 hours and just write; ½ an hour, maybe an hour was max. That wasn't going to cut it... But it was a long enough time interval of focus to write poetry, though. The period as I was finally leaving academia was my most creative time for poetry. It was a poem I wrote during my last semester at school, and I think while on cold medicine did I write it—this was the first writing I ever officially got published. It was a small (literally, it was physically the size of one sheet of paper folded over, as well as it not being a high volume publication) literary magazine named, *Dirigible,* and I was the first poem in issue #11. Yeah, 11. Heh. Here it is:

"An Ether"

Last night I dined with afterimages
of angels, in whose minds
I was the quotient of their imaginations.
We were served emotions by maids
whose faces were mirrors, and we
ate until only distance remained.
The flavor of despair was akin
to blood, like iron ground into nothing,
only a tingle that something once was.

Solitude tasted of a star grown cold,
reminded me of the air of Autumn
where the leaves had all fallen,
complete, yet yearning. Anger
was the strongest rum pressure
could distill, it churned in my belly
like a violent wave disbelieving its
confinement. And our dessert was joy,
yellow sprouts of light which had
the savor of a tickle, and was gone
before the tongue had finished
tasting. Afterwards, the Book of Life
was opened, and every name
written therein danced ethereally
above the pages and then rained
into my soul to give me new breath.
The air, now heavy with promises,
folded, again and again and again and
again, until finally, being nothing,
everything was as the moment
before creation, empty and perfect.

All good, things were, right? Living the American dream? Well… this was when I entered a situation at that point that I had not prepared for. It was not a bad thing, per se, but something you wouldn't expect. It was a simple, everyday thing: I was told, "Good job." If I remember right, it was not so much a thing that happened when you were a student. You got grades, and they were sort of abstract things, in fact pretty small things in comparison to the effort you put into that "A". But when I was starting work, they were saying things like, "Nice work" or even "Excellent", and if it was done right proper, it was due to some significant effort that was well performed. So, where was the problem?

See, I'll tell you that the problem was, well, I was the fuckup—if you'll excuse my French. For so long, I couldn't do *anything* right. So, I heard the words, that told me I had done something good, something of value, and peripherally I understood the meaning of the words; but no, I didn't really *get* them. They were as if of a language half foreign, and they bounced off my brain without transferring any kind of the fundamental meaning that normals took for granted when they heard things like that, when were informed of such sentiment. And it took a long time for me to come around on this....

I was working for a .com company, and this was 1998—during the internet boom—and it was San Francisco (practically ground zero of the phenomenon). It was all so thrilling. We all thought we were going to be *rich*. We didn't know at that point only 1 startup in 20 was going to make it. At this point in my timeline there was a bit of turbulence as far as drugs were concerned: I was trying to quit the ganja. I would go months without the barest puff, then I would go to Haight St. and pick up a bag or two and smoke like a fiend for like 2 weeks. I was a Jekyll and Hyde.

Interestingly, whenever I took my first hit after a longish drought (I think 7 months was the longest for that time period), it was often a traumatic experience. There was once I had a paranoid fantasy, once I took a couple inhales, that "they" were reading my mind, from a helicopter above my apartment—they knew where I lived! I could almost hear the beating of the rotors. I looked out my window, and I looked up, and I could swear I could see a helicopter, hovering above! I couldn't believe it. That is, I refused to believe it, and I still do. Nothing came of it, however, no men in black came down on a rope from above. I am convinced that that was the biggest hallucination I ever had. Makes me almost believe in UFO abductions.

At the job, as I was saying, I was doing quite well. I almost had a girlfriend in an attractive female who also worked there, but I came on a little too strong with my Christianity on our first quasi-date type thing (that was humming along, too—churchgoing Catholic I was). In the course of my "good job," I was promoted a few times, and I was making more money than I knew what to do with. Seriously, if you suddenly stop doing drugs all the time, the cash just piles up. It is a strange thing, indeed.

In the last ½ year that I worked there, though, *the stress.* OMG. I had a ½ hour walk to work every morning—beautiful, through the streets of San Francisco, the land of eternal spring. And every morning, as I walked, I would think, *"Please* let a car hit me today!" Not to kill me, mind you, and I wouldn't take any stupid risks along the way, but just to lay me up in the hospital for a little while, where I wouldn't have to think about my project at all. (I always liked going to hospitals. On the outside, I have a thousand cares; inside, my only worry, my only job is to get well.)

And I remember the exact moment the internet bubble burst. It was spring 2000. I was watching CNBC, I think it was, and they announced that the Justice Department was not dropping its antimonopoly suit against Microsoft. The next day, NASDAQ dropped like 200 points, and it was never the same after that. That summer, one of those days, I saw that my project manager looked kinda down. I asked him about it and he said that he had lost $100,000 the day before, in the stock market. Yeesh. Myself, I lost maybe a total of $10,000 throughout the whole downturn. I consider myself lucky.

And that company I was working for? They blew through $48 million in 2 years. They had gone from 30 to 250 employees in a year and a half, because that's what bubbles do: they inflate. They would rent out a building twice a year, once for the anniversary party, once for the Christmas party. Free bar, always. They knew how to party, if nothing else. I quit in May of 2001, after having been as stressed as I wrote about above. They were then broke soon after, and couldn't raise a cent more to fuel the train they were riding. It was the end of an era, and not just for me. A pretty wild time for anyone near the epicenter, though I guess I got the tame side of the whole experience. I didn't get invited to most of the wild parties; I was already starting to get a reputation as a kind of goody-two-shoes quiet religious guy. But yeah, there was a wild time to come in my book of days, in the next few months, alone in my San Francisco studio apartment—at the end of which the angels decided to kick my ass.

7 Book of Beginnings

I was so burned out after the .com crash. For the next 3 months I got stoned and played video games. There was nothing productive going on, as far as the real world was concerned. I was living off the remainder of the savings which I had squirreled away, a bunch of which had been put into a mutual fund which started going south almost the moment I decided to invest in it, during the second half of my gainful employment. Pot, video games, and I visited the massage parlor a bunch of times. And then, since the medical insurance was tied to the job, I ran out of meds, out of Zyprexa. Things were poised for an Episode.

I remember one time during the months of decompression that I had a vision of Hell, and a vision of Heaven. Didn't feel much of their experience, but got an idea of what they must be like. It was more like a vision of their infrastructure, not their environment. There was also this time I made Rosanna Arquette faint. And Joan of Arc gave me little kisses all over my face once, I did not comprehend just why she would want to that, at the time. I also received the Holy Spirit maybe for the third time. Now I was neither the Archangel Michael, nor (most of the time) the Beast 666. I made sense some of the time, if I recall correctly, and other times the context to what I spoke spoke of a personal weird. I was now a third thing, other than angel or beast: one of the 2 witnesses of the Apocalypse, written about in chapter 11 of the Book of Revelation.

This idea had occurred to me before, in fact—upon having been busted out with everyone else from the Black Iron Prison, back when I stopped for the while from thinking I was literally the second coming of Jesus Christ. Meeting God does things to you, even *thinking* you have met God does things to you. Being now a servant of the Most High, I looked in Revelation and found chapter 11 immediately, and thought I was going to be that. I don't know why that struck me, then. But I did later think of why that would have been so cool: the position(s) had yet to be filled, there's only 2 of them in the whole history of the universe, and *it's in the Bible!*

So, once while I was in church at St. Patrick's in San Francisco, I signaled to the higher ups, "Here am I." This is what Isaiah said when the powers that be asked, "Whom shall we send?" Now, this far along, now that I had gotten somewhere in my life and was a productive member of society, I was allowed to believe that Rosanna Arquette and I were they, the Two Witnesses of the Apocalypse. In fact, I wrote on my blog, "Romeo and Juliet witness the Apocalypse!" (That's who we were.) It's still there, on my blog, dated to when the angels decided to kick my ass.

You might be wondering what the deal is with Rosanna Arquette. I mentioned it before, with *The Princess Bride:* it was supposed to be true love. But true love, at least, according to Arquette, the term meant something else completely—especially since she was an actor: nothing short of *Romeo & Juliet.* And I must admit, it is a potent potion, that star-crossed tale.

All my young life, I looked for the love of my dreams. The one. Soulmate. True love. Don't get me wrong, it's not that I've never had love—make no mistake—but nothing that would be sufficient for all my years—and I know it's possible, to find that specific one. Then, ever since my life had become epic in so many cool and weird and sticky and harsh and blissful ways, it was not a quest just to find that special one, but to find in the world to be able to wrap myself in the garments of destiny itself: true, true love. I had no idea at this point that true love was actually impossible, and that this fact was built into the fabric of creation. This was of the dissonant thread that Melkor wove into the music of the Ainur, the junking of the works when Lucifer threw a monkey wrench into the system.

All I thought for years was that true love was Rosanna Arquette. (Kallisti! The Apple of Discord was meant for the prettiest.) How did she fit into all this, with the personages of history, the angels, and the War? Nowhere, really. She was a civilian. But for years, she and I were an item. At least, in my head. When I thought I was Michael, we (the congregation inside my head) then theorized that archangels appeared in pairs, and that she was an unknown angel named Michelle (Michael and Michelle, to go with Gabriel and Gabrielle, and of course, Lucifer and Lucifera). And when we played that real people could be the epitome of Shakespeare characters, then, we were Romeo and Juliet. Like, the *real* Romeo and Juliet. Who witness the Apocalypse.

Years later, when I found my actual true love, that true love at every point along the way expected the other shoe to drop, and that I would leave her and go back to Arquette. Yes, Arquette and I had been together for that long. But no, it wasn't going to happen. I got disenchanted with her, somewhere along the way, even after forgiving that thing with the urination, or lack thereof. I told her, when I got to the point where I was walking the streets of New York City, that *R & J* had been just a chapter in my life, and I had turned the page.

She had a problem letting go, I think, especially when I got to be heroic, in a sense: one of those worthy to be among the Heavenly Host, let us say. This was in my head of course, but that's where she was. But true love—I never closed the door to that, even when things got dark, or even when things got ordinary. The latter is more dangerous than the former. It is what everyone has been searching for when they ask of the cold, dark sky, "What is the purpose of it all? What is the meaning of life?" It makes sense of a lifetime's pain. Yes, we have love, the world's saving grace, and God is love, but *true love,* destiny you can hold and press up against... that's next level to the next level. And if anyone on Earth ever has known true love, I ask, why do we still ask what the meaning of life is?

Arquette... I did have it bad for she whom I thought was Her, during the while. I even bought a ticket to go to LA, to go and ring her bell (literally, not figuratively), because you know, who knows? Maybe impossible things can happen. But before I could go, August 26, 2001 happened.

I smoked some pot—the last I ever would—then went for a walk. Then the angels made the world... not the world. They played with the filters on the camera, as it were, and once again, I was dreaming while I was awake. They convinced me that I had just been a part of the Rapture, and what I was seeing that looked like San Francisco was actually Heaven—just that it looked like Earth as a transition step to actually seeing Heaven all around me. And so I was to take off all my clothes, as to remove all attachments to the former world. And so I did. What on Earth happened, you may ask? You may guess, what I did was walk around San Francisco naked. For about ½ an hour, I wandered around, asking anyone I would meet if they had any spare clothes—'cause you know, everything in Heaven is free.

Needless to say, the police picked me up from off the street, and they set me up in the psych ward at San Francisco General. In one of those orange jumpsuits, to cover me up, which I must say was surprisingly comfortable. The time there in SF general was pretty uneventful. I remember reading the Book of Ecclesiastes and thinking that if I had read and understood it when I was younger, I would have saved myself mountains of grief. And then two weeks later, when they let me out, I moved out of my little apartment in the city to stay instead with my brother, and others, at a house in Albany (California) they were renting. I had stopped smoking anything.

A couple months in, I would begin my seminal project: artificial intelligence. (I spent many an hour on it, from October of 2001 to December 2012. In fact, I once calculated/estimated that I spent 12,000 hours on it, about. At that point, the Event happened. Upended my world.) And in this course, I got ready for a day when a wing and a prayer became my normal mode of being. I was making my mind up to be a good man. I remember hearing the voice of the Lord tell Michael, when I moved into Albany, "Looks like we have a straggler in our midst!" Yeah, that would be me.

So that was where I ended up. I don't remember anything earth shattering happening there in that house (at least, not in my head). I think having multiple roommates might have had something to do with that; I almost never was completely alone. Early on, recovering and getting back on the Zyprexa, there were these dappled fuzzy moments when I couldn't tell if I were alive or had died and gone to Heaven. That was maybe the strangest of what happened at that place.

There was this one time that I was Spider-Man in a dream, then exactly when I woke up, the song "Hero" came on the radio (which was the theme song for the movie). And then, 9/11 happened when I was living there. My brother tried to wake me up more than once, but only when he said, "thousands of people are dead!" did he get me out of bed. It was surreal, watching that second plane crash into the second tower again and again through the day. It was as if I were watching a movie, but man, it was *real*. I won't go into that any more, I'm sure you know all about it. It didn't trigger anything bizarre in my head.

I got a job in early 2002 and then in 2003 I was so stressed out by it I started smoking again (cigarettes). I still miss smoke. Did I do any strange things during that mini-era? What went on in my head? Rosanna Arquette was there, now and again, and I was still mildly tripping (from 1991), but I was mostly on the down low. I OD'ed on cough medicine once, and I had a sort of drug trip, and I thought I was damned. Again. What's to tell? It was a pretty normal life, though outside my roommates I had little social contact. I gained a lot of weight in the first few months of my time there, and then I lost ½ of it a little while more into my stay. (Quitting smoking usually means weight gain, after all.)

I started to go deep into the problem of AI, doing research in every spare moment, sleeping for 12 hours on Friday and Saturday nights, then all day and night Saturday and Sunday doing research. Even more: I wrote a book. I don't know where I found the time. I wrote *The Sinner's Prayer Book,* a resource for the lost.

Then there was this which was related to my AI research, when I came up with my twofold metaphysics: everything, everywhere, real or imagined, can be described as the yin and yang of information and structure (actually, should be yang and yin). When I was talking to Einstein about this, I said, "If you try and see structure, you will only see information," and he followed, "So if you try and see information, you will see structure," to which I said, "No, you can never see structure. You will only ever see information." And you know what? He never forgave me for one-upping him there. Also, there was something I saw, when I corrected him that one time, barely perceptible; I only realized I had seen it years on from then. It was a black dot. The implications of it came farther down the river. [See Appendix: Walt Disney Is God]

The workload at the place I was programming started to become heavier then. And my parents tried to set me up with this woman (Korean) who lived in Kansas. And she was going to be in Seoul for the summer, so I visited Korea in July of 2003. There, I was walking around Insadong, a "traditional" part of the city, and it was as if I heard my ancestors calling me. Back in the Bay Area, I was getting tired of being stressed out, working long days and weekends. But now, drawing from how I had felt I was being called, I had a dawning of realization: I could say goodbye to all of this, and go teach English in Korea. What could I do then but start planning this departure? Away from the country, from the stress, from the same old thing? This was about August.

I'm not one to burn bridges, so I stayed long enough to wrap things up, as far as what I was working on involved. But this was a one-way ticket (for at least the near future), and by November I had quit/left my job, quit smoking anything for good, and I was off to Seoul, Korea, to find what I could of adventure there. What could possibly go wrong? It was to be another beginning.

Perhaps this is a book of beginnings? They are well worth the ink that marks them. Shall we pursue this path now? Beginnings are sorts of mysterious things, and only one of them had nothing ending before it, that anyone could understand. Or was there was something, even there? We could go back to where we started this whole thing and try and stitch a couple myths together—a Frankenmyth. It is said that Lucifer begot Sin, correct? How, exactly? Milton wrote that she came directly from his forehead, like Athena from Zeus's head. But why would that have happened? You know, I have my own idea about that: simply put, he said "No" to the Holy Spirit.

To blaspheme against the Holy Spirit is what Christ said was the unforgivable sin, and the Lord himself told me that that is done by saying "no" to Him. For to say no to love's will means that that part of you is no more. Love asks of you only good things, that of life. If that part of you is gone, there may still be motion to it, but it is basically flamed out. He was the first to have ever done this, Lucifer was, and it was complete, an utter denial of all that love was, in him. Thus came to be from that first and greatest of evil, the Evil that he made of himself: he did what we call Sin. And as Sin was forming, when the Holy Spirit was to give light, to give life to her—for Lucifer's action had such consequence in Heaven—she was killed, out of mercy.

To have given the light of life to the darkness that had gained form from Lucifer's action would have been to create a creature who would only have known (excruciating) pain. So she was slain before she could be born. Which meant she was denied life—but she could not exactly die because there was no death that was in primordial existence before her. Thus she still does move as if life were in her, and gives birth to monsters. This was the one whom Philip K. wrote about, the one whom we all lament—because she never got a chance.

Now, there was another myth regarding Lucifer, one where he had had first go in creation, and that the dinosaurs were his failed try in his own action of creation. But what if we modify that, and go back to before "Let there be light," and look at Tiamat/Rahab, if you recall these? What if Sin, who was slain, were the one whose body it was that was the watery chaos, back when in Genesis the Earth was said to be formless and void? Because it was as if he buried that body in the soil from which all our world sprang. And this was Lucifer "salting the earth," as it were: to make the creating of anything in such a matrix impossible, thinking not with the understanding that with God, nothing is impossible. The Lord brought light and life into the cosmos anyway, but what Lucifer did had profound effect on how anything happened, how everything worked.

That's my own, original myth, what I've been able to piece together in my experiences—with the visions going to and fro, leaving meaning behind. You know, it's strange what people leave lying around sometimes, with a slip of the wrist. Stranger still, one might believe, would be what God leaves lying around—with a wink and a smile.

8 Neighboring Halospace

The spirits I saw were a thorny issue. (These spirits of people who were alive… how was I seeing the actual people?) That I was in contact with the Dreaming was a tempting solution, right? Perhaps it did solve everything, rationally: I saw the people you meet in dreams, that my dream mechanism had broken. Originally I was so out of it I thought I was somehow talking to the actual people on Earth, if they were still kicking around. Logic wasn't a prerequisite to my theories at that point. I did drive from Philly to New York a couple times right when my mind had exploded, after all, because Rosanna Arquette had told me that she was going to meet me there. I thought for a long time, too, that she would one of these days pick me up from wherever I happened to be. I was a dude in distress, awaiting rescue. And that, of course, never happened.

So, what then? Were they just part and parcel of madness, schizophrenia's fruit? This, perhaps, is the easiest to believe, especially to anyone who are in the "I don't believe in any of this stuff" camp. I thought in the early days that I was looking into an alternate dimension, but that made little sense, itself. I wasn't thinking that clearly at that point. Once I posited that only *some* of the people I saw were real: the angels and the Lord, but not Albert Einstein nor Rosanna Arquette: these were entity-like creations made by said angels. Like shadow puppets. Which still left the question of what exactly I was looking into. Halospace, right? What the heck was it?

I have a theory, now, about the situation, but it requires a bit of suspension of disbelief. If you've come this far, you're probably set in that department, whether you believe the things I say or at least find my thinking entertaining. Here we go. Let's say, technically, you don't exist in the world that is seen. We are, as the Police song says, spirits in the material world (which comes from the writings of Arthur Koestler). We exist only in Eternity, the unseen world. The interface of the spirit with the body comprises the mind, or soul, or psyche. And that's usually it, all that we're used to. But imagine, now, your spirit able to look into the unseen world. It's like looking within, but more accurately, this is to see by your third eye, which is called your *ajna* eye. All of whoever existed, or will exist, are now accessible, since we're talking about looking into Eternity, which encloses all things. The experience of Eternity while still earthbound: this is the Halospace.

There's more. Hell, or what I call the unfair Hell, exists. But it is not an eternal place. It is like an eternity, with time outside of the visible world operating in it, but it, too, will be thrown into the Lake of Fire at the Last Judgement. So it is in this part of Eternity that the "bad guys" hail from, when I contact them in the Halospace. And since this, and all Halospace time is not the same as the time on Earth, thus I can speak to Rosanna Arquette and she has no idea of it while still in the world. For the spirits to talk to me enter the context around me, not the context of their own earthly forms.

Halospace, last we left off, was pretty quiet for me. But it was still there, just around the psyche's corner, as if perhaps I took just one wrong turn… it would be upon me like a robber on the road. Indeed, my "visits" to Halospace, or the "episodes" I would have were the reason I lost many an article of curiosity—books mostly, as my pragmatics were fizzled out when that other world took over, and I concerned myself very little with keeping what material things I had. Things took on a different value during the episodes, things merely a means to an end, nothing really precious but the deeds that I would do.

Time catches up with you if you don't make the effort to catch up with it, that is, the world. November 7, 2003 was when I quit smoking, and I think it was the next day when I got on my flight to Korea. Yeah, I was leaving it all behind. (Quite literally in one sense: a lot of the stuff I left behind with "trusted" people ended up disappearing by the time I got back.) In a month from landing, I got myself a job, at a place called Pagoda, as an English teacher. I really had needed to get away from the technology sector for a while. It was at Pagoda where I met Eunhye (pronounced, roughly, "unhay").

In the first time she walked in the classroom door, instant and mutual attraction. I found out as the class progressed she knew and liked Bob Marley, and she played drums for fun. In fact, I found she had the best taste in music of anyone I'd ever met. (Read: most like mine.) She seemed so cool. Sharp as a tack and everything. But I did wait until she was no longer my student before asking her out. Honorable, you know?

For a few months there, I had it all. A fun job teaching English; and separately real meaning in the AI research, that I loved to do; a babe for a girlfriend; and peace in the Lord. Read what I wrote in my blog during those days:

> I am living someone else's life. This is not me. I am a madman huddled in an out of the way corner somewhere, imagining all this. I don't know whose persona I borrowed, but this assumed identity is too capable, is too sure of himself, is too good. Surely I am not able to do these things I do—it is a sweet dream, and perhaps one day I will awake to the real whatever I am. But until that day, I will play the game like I know what I'm doing, live this life as if it were my very own. I should not ques-

tion this simulacrum, though I know I sometimes will: I will wonder if, I will wonder how, and I will wonder why. When the real owner of this soul comes back to claim it, I will not contend with him; I will just smile as I give it back, and thank him for such a lovely day out in the sun. [2/20/04]

    I understood why there was a reason why that phrase became so popular back when: "You complete me."[xi] At least, to my reckoning. St. Paul said that if one could, to be celibate as he was, but that it was better to marry than to burn with passion. But we can trace this advice to his belief that the Lord was, by his calculations, coming back any day now. He writes it more than once in the letters of his to various churches, which make up a bulk of the New Testament. It was actually a big issue to the early Christians, when they started dying off and Christ still had not returned. That issue was even written of in the New Testament, in a letter that Paul probably did not write but was ascribed to him.
    One can only imagine what his advice might have been if he had known the world would stick around for so long after, because, you know, it has that nasty habit of not ending. Myself, if I were a saint, I would be at odds (so to speak) against a major percentage of my brothers and sisters in Christ, and I would recommend coupling up. We're not going anywhere for a long time, as in, the Lord's not returning in your lifetime, your children's lifetime, or your grandchildren's lifetime. As I have said, we are in the coming of the Oasis (we in the 1st world, at least, still to go how to bring the rest of the world to be like we are), and desert living doesn't apply anymore. We have come to the table of plenty: the means and free time enough to go on the great quest of our age: to find a soulmate. Because that kind of love brings together the above with the below, and it is not blasphemy to say that to

know someone that closely is another type of holy. Whole, when what you were missing was something that you didn't know what it was, because you never had it before. Only stories. Until you suddenly had it. And you found yourself complete.

I was with Eunhye from January to October. We did a lot of walking around the city and going to movies. Neither of us had been big on dating before. I look back and I think I wish I'd have thought of more things to do, but hindsight, you know? By late summer her job was stressing her out, and I was running low on medication (I was taking a quarter of one pill a day). I started zoning out on our dates, and she got fed up with me, I suppose. Everything in her life was going to pot. She put me at such a distance that it ended up that *I* broke up with *her*. When I had first met her, she had quit smoking and drinking, but by the end of our time, she was back with both of them again. This saga does continue. Later.

I was as yet still not really normal; I was not experiencing things like you'd think someone as normal-seeming as me should. Another little blog entry a bit after the breakup:

> Sometimes I still have moments of unreality. I recall this happened every now and again when I was going out with my last girlfriend: something about the what I experienced did not seem like it was a genuine one, a feeling like it was merely a simulation of life, that on a deeper level, it was not really happening. What am I comparing these things with, I wonder? Where did I ever get a sense of what a fundamental ground of existence might be, that which is more solid than the most solid of all material things? For that is what the unreality centers on: these things are too light to

be true, that there is something deeper elsewhere I am sensing in my subconscious, which I cannot quite put my finger on, but somehow I know it is there.

It comes sometimes just as I'm walking down the street. Not even the asphalt seems to be as solid as all that, that there is nothing that truly fills it with reality. Everything is hollow. Somewhere I have lost the sense of that which exists, it would seem, that there is a malfunctioning circuit in the experiencing of anything—that life is like a waking dream, with no girding of fundamental soundness to it. I half expect at times that all things will halt and its true nature, its hidden nature, will reveal itself... though it never does, of course. I do not know what it is that I have to get used to make the real things seem real. Things are real enough, for now, but the hints of madness I don't know if they will ever let me get past the shadow of doubt, that this is really happening, that life is truly here.
[11/7/04]

It was not just that I spoke with angels, which I thought to be real. That might be a delusional thing that one expects someone who is mentally weird would experience. It was that, at least at times, *reality* didn't seem to be real. At some level I knew it was, by the grace of the Lord. But it was like that what we see all around us is an illusion: very Buddhist, though not with the same approach vector. I was going in the opposite direction from Siddhartha, from the illusion to find the reality in it, from the hollowness, the solidity. And I found out it sort of sneaks on you, what we expect to be normal. I mean, when things gradually seemed solid again. You forget how things were so wrong. For life goes on.

After Eunhye and I broke up, the matchmaking engine of the elders revved up. If I had been 20 years younger, I would have said "adults" instead of "elders". You know, mom, dad, aunts and uncles. Yeah, the parents and aunt (whom I was living with, once again) just set me up on first date after first date after first date. I would see 3 women a week, once 3 women in a day. I think I saw 75 of them in 2005. I liked maybe 3 of them. None of which dating did they go anywhere. It was entertaining, at least, though—to other people. I remember Bob at least was a regular visitor to my blog at that time, and only at that time. To me it was a chore, like doing the dishes. So many first dates...

I did get back on the medication. My aunt set me up with a doctor who would prescribe it for me, and it was about a 3rd of the price than in the 'States. So I went from 0 to 60 again in my intake. And such a huge increase in Zyprexa in the blood, unfortunately, meant weight gain. Which wouldn't have been *too* bad, except that I happened to run into Eunhye at this Starbucks, months later. After I had gained all sorts of weight. And we were talking again, phoning each other, but she couldn't get over that weight issue, how that made me look, and she just wanted to be friends. Which I couldn't stand for, so I broke up with her again. You can call me a pig if you want, the heart wants what it wants.

I wrote a short story about it. In it, I relate how in October 2001, while I was still a little tweaked (from the episode where I walked around naked), I wanted to see the face of my wife, and had a small vision of a woman's face. Years later, after Eunhye and I had been dating for a couple three months, she looked up at me from a certain angle... and it was *her!* So I was confused, both times when I broke up with her. Wasn't this the woman whom, after the first date, I thought, "This is the girl I'm going to marry"? WTF? But it wasn't done, not yet—there would be more. Later. Weird things were still afoot.

Back when I was low on meds, around when Eunhye and I had broken up the first time, I had a weird vision of me in Heaven. Apparently I did or was going to do something worthwhile, and I was famous there. I had long hair, like I did when my mind exploded around age 22, and the same kind of clothes. I believe I was wearing this tie dye shirt with a picture of Rasta Mickey (Mouse) on it that I had long since lost, somewhere along the way, here on Earth. Perhaps you find in Heaven everything you lost while kicking around down here?

Along that time, with that sort of vision, I had the attacks of the usual delusion, that I was the Antichrist, yada yada yada. I had to tell my aunt that I hadn't done any drugs; I'm sure she was acutely worried about that. And it was a first, I think: I didn't do anything *stupid* while being "in my head" somewhat, my eyes in Halospace. I think the worst of it may have been when I got a little lost looking for this hill trail my aunt and I frequented, but I found my way eventually. I did get introspective, now and again. Here's a blog entry from then:

> I am still haunted, sometimes, by things that never happened. Did I ever tell you that I sent my father to Hell, once? Or that I sent a troop of Koreans into a well of pain as huge as the sun? And my once hero, Jimi Hendrix, I saw him disintegrate and did nothing to stop it, back when I believed myself all-powerful. When I thought Micha-el the Archangel lost the War in Heaven, I showed my purest cowardice, letting anyone and everyone fill that role instead of me. I wanted to be Lucifer Morningstar, God's brightest angel, but one who never fell from

grace. I thought I was the Antichrist who wanted nothing to do with evil. I praised Hitler, tried to save him on more than one occasion (my intent was good, for if he could be saved, could not anyone? though we all know all about where good intentions are the road to). They were just pictures in my head, but I thought it was all so real while it was happening. And I was no hero, given even the countless chances to live up to the hype I was pumping myself with for so long.

I wonder sometimes what these things say about my true nature. I always thought myself one of the good guys, but maybe I just wanted to be on the side that I was sure that won. And we have been taught from so far back that the good guys always do win in the end.... Perhaps I am a little too hard on myself, though these bad things are easier to remember than any small good I may have accomplished to the people floating in my head. Yes, yes: I was messed up; I understand that. That seems of little comfort though, when you believe yourself in possession of the knowledge of what you are capable of, if it came right down to it. I guess, though, if I really try, I can count it all joy. I know what a wretch I was—still am, to at least some degree (I am certain). Given a second chance to prove myself, knowing that what is happening really is happening: second chances like that are few and far between. This second chance of mine (third, and fourth, I sometimes think), I pray I don't blow it. And there are some God given fibers

in me that believe—I know not why—that I won't.
[10/5/04]

It's one thing to have dreams, and to follow a dream. It's quite another to be caught up in a dream that has you, that you are merely the way it enters the world. You gain a sense of perspective when you see how small a cog you are in the whole scheme, that is—if you need a name for it—Eternity. And that's how fairy tales end, right? "And they lived happily ever after." That might be the dream worth following, perhaps above all the rest of them.

9 Busyness

Time is a thief that steals itself. Even when you get a second chance, you do not go back in time to restart your decision process. That time is gone. Ever since the Lord had called me a "straggler", I stopped wasting any time, for the most part. All during the whole Eunhye drama I was still working on my AI, whenever I could. It all started originally in a notion I had to work at a game company, on game AI. I had thought perhaps the cutting edge of AI lay there. So I drew up plans for a game, to showcase the new AI I would be developing. It was some sort treatment of airplanes dogfighting. A little while into it, I realized it wasn't going to be feasible.

I didn't really play games, usually, and when I did, nowhere near enough to understand in my gut what would fly and what would sink in their design. All the information about games I had was basically academic. So then I had another idea, of combining the two main branches of AI: the connectionist (or "scruffy", like neural networks) and the symbolic (or "neat", like regular natural language processing). I coined the word "metaron", supposedly short for "meta-neuron", as a goal in the project (a metaron net/work). Then I took it to the next level.

I began to question all of what had gone on before me in this field, that I could find and seemed interesting to me, and what were the frontiers that were currently being explored. And I found the ideas of emergence and self-organizing systems fascinated me. Emergence is where the whole is greater than the sum of its parts, like you wouldn't be able to tell from a single neuron that when you hooked a lot of them together, intelligence would form. Intelligence would emerge. And self-organizing systems means what's on the tin. I thought about these two conceptual areas a lot, and I printed out research paper after research paper on these topics, most of which I didn't use in any real way. How could one make something emerge? How could one create a catalyst for self-organizing systems? I didn't realize at the time that what I had been following was the wrong approach, that if indeed you succeeded in both those goals, the emergent self-organizing system you'd end up with is a nest of termites, or an ant hill. Not the way to go.

Fortunately, I was sent in another direction. Before I had this big idea, my research was a lot of 5 steps forward, 4 steps back. I would start going in one direction, then I would think of an exception that invalidated almost all that I had come up with. Such was the nature of the beast. Then, finally, in 2004 I had an epiphany, which could be written in a quasi-equation:

$$\text{information} = \Delta \text{potential}$$

Or in words, information is a change in potential. Further, in line with that idea, measurement is a change in information. Change being creation, destruction or transformation. And after I came up with these, there was no turning back.

Then, I was given something in a dream, too. Right before I woke up one morning, I saw a node, a circle drawn on a piece of paper, and an arrow from that node going to another node. And (holy cow!) it hit me: meaning is a change in state. (The Lord would take credit for this inspiration. It was a Christmas present.) It was another manifestation of my theory—information was a change in potential in this form of representation. I was really going the right way. It was quite a year, 2004.

It would be still years till I wrote a single line of code, but this, the most basic of foundations, was possibly most important of my breakthroughs. I could not have built anything without it. That was not all of it, though. At certain points I have thought that I had every large concept worked out and in the bag, and every time was I mistaken. And even when I did get something big nailed down, the devil was certainly in the details. Where the rubber hits the road, something actually solid has to be there, not a tire that liquefies and slips away when you try and give it some gas.

I loved research. Around that time, when I was in Seoul, mostly it would consist of going to a big bookstore, getting some coffee, and wandering around thinking and sipping that coffee. I always had a little pad of paper on me when I went. And I was seeing if there were any interesting books to buy. If I bought a $100 book, and it helped me solve one problem along the way, I'd consider that well bought. What is it worth, if it can resolve some logic I needed? Not just books about computers, or even mathematics, but some of the best stuff were in books of *architecture.* I have thought that I missed my true calling, back when I was in the right position to decide such things. I read about the foundations of architecture and the mixture of art and science tickled all the right mental muscles. Oh, well. Maybe next lifetime. (What? What do you mean we just get one? Worst video game ever.)

Now the years ticked on by. 2005 was a very normal year. I don't remember it that well. If I put my mind on it, I have memories not hazy, but—ones that didn't sink in properly. Not any weight to them. The lack of memory was not for any reason that I used to might have had, like sophomore year. I seem to have one main memory of *that* year: sitting in Bob and Scott's dorm room with Led Zeppelin cranked up to 11, passing around a pipe. That wacky tobaccy. But no, never again. Well, maybe if they legalize it in New York. And then, *maybe.* But I digress.

2005 I do seem to recall a lot of those first dates, and then after breaking up with Eunhye a second time, I started working out and working on my gut. Research was going swimmingly, where I coined the term "radiplex networks". I mention it because it just sounds cool. I started working for my friend Chris, who was CEO of his company, and who was going out with my brother's ex-girlfriend. (That was how I knew him.) But to one who has had some harrowing times, the lack of intensity of this year was probably its most prominent feature. And you know what? I should probably be thankful for that. Half the time the world is ending,[xii] after all. I got a breather.

Another tick. 2006 was a bit of a thrill. I was talking to Chris that I was getting a little stir crazy holed up in my aunt's house all the livelong day, and I was going to quit. So then he found me possible assignment to work in New York City, and I said that'll do. I would need a new computer, having owned the one I was using for 6 years. This was back when Apple was releasing their first Intel based Macs. And I was thinking that I was just getting used to living in Korea, and I half wished it wouldn't gel, but it did, and I went. Staying in a hotel, I had only a week to find an apartment after I embarked on this new adventure. There was one apartment listing where I went to take a look, and this lady and I went up to the place; and I swear, she had split a studio apartment into three sections—and she was renting out one of those sections for $1300 a month. I sat there on the bed that filled most of the section she was trying to rent to me, whereupon I seriously said to her, "Listen, I stay in a lot, and I think if I lived here, I would go insane."

I did find a really good apartment though, like a stroke of fate. The job I was assigned to was a bank, so some websites were verboten there, including the primary resource for such things, Craig's List. Which I still am puzzled by, why that site would be blocked. Maybe it was the hookers section, back when, when they still had one? So anyway, because of the said censorship, I hap-

89

pened to find a not as popular website called Sublets.com. There I found the place I'm living in still, now. The forces converged on Thursday in the week I had to find a place. I remember getting out of the subway to look at the place for the first time: Barnes & Noble right out of the subway exit, Starbucks on that same block, then post office across the street from the apartment. They were all in the space of 3 short blocks. I remember thinking, just then, "I'm home." And I didn't even know about the supermarket or the IMAX movie theater!

Things were as normal as could be expected. I had a semi-crazy story about when I landed at JFK about when we boarded a shuttle/van to go to Philadelphia. I was going to see my mother, whom I hadn't seen the whole time I was in Korea. Before I found the van, in fact, the second I got out of customs, some guy asks if I needed a taxi. I told him I was going to use the van service, and he kinda grunted that it was not running anymore. Which was a lie, and I have no idea what he stood to gain by saying so. So when we all, a group of us, got onto said van, there was a hint of some funk. The bad kind. Someone was (it seemed) traveling with a bag full of dirty, smelly socks. The whole trip—that was the focal point of the whole 2 hours we were driving. At one point someone put on some cologne, and we had a temporary respite, but then the funk just strong-armed any other smell out of existence. Welcome back to America, eh?

Normal as I lived, I was still having experiences in the Halo-space, or maybe you could say I was just not rooted very solidly in this thing we agree upon as reality. Blog from that same year:

> There are still times, they come and go, when I half expect the world to turn inside out, reveal its hidden, horrible face. Then the unutterable truth would be revealed, and I would be shown to my-

self and the world in the light of all darkness: yes, even these days, I still half think that this might just happen, almost peeking out from behind the veil of ordinary life. I regain my senses, though, always, never letting myself believe it all the way—not even close to it, really—the feeling passes like a whim of the wind. There will always be perhaps things that reason will not penetrate, at least, not to their full depths, always a ghost somewhere in the machine, a bit of beast in the most civilized countenances. I imagine this little wildness in the plain face of the universe does me some good, somewhere. Maybe just as a reminder that things are not always as they seem, and that one's whole life might turn on the thinnest dime. [12/21/06]

And sometimes, nowadays, I forget that I once was hanging by a thread. And that on occasion, that thread broke, and I would have to climb back up there, into the clear air. I would have to reestablish the context of reality to my shaken psyche. But it was not to dip so very far into the Hells, for much in any of the falls was firstly through the Heavens I had climbed up to.

I suppose I was stable enough in those days. I call the effect, "the doomsday clock that never rang." I have mentioned this before. The poem I get that from is below. One may expect there exists somewhere a cataclysm waiting around some corner; but it's never there, whichever corner you take. By induction one must conclude that the doomsday clock will never ring. Because when all the conditions seemed to point to it happening seemed to have been flipped on, nothing. Nada. The world didn't end… again. And so you just carry on.

Around this time did I think, now, that I was stable enough to start my own company, based on the AI I hadn't as yet written a single line of code for. All I did have was a hodge podge of vague assertions. And as according to Bertrand Russell, "Everything is vague to a degree you do not realize till you have tried to make it precise." I would find this harsh reality out the hard way. But near the end of 2006, I swallowed the germ that I was getting a little tired of the rat race, even if it was a pretty cushy one. You know, all things considered. I was going to call my company Eonwing LLC, and I remember I had to jump through a couple hoops to get that "LLC" part. I owned eonwing.com, of course, and I designed the logo based on a dragonfly wing, and playing around on Photoshop. Our mascot was therefore the dragonfly. Paperwork was filed. All of the above, these devices that I worked in the real world were how I indeed felt removed from the pale cast of madness:

"Out of Madness"

Scratches on the mirror lose the certainty of pattern;
the underlying randomness peeks through.
The voice which speaks in silent, profound meaning
fades into the horizon as the distance from divine purpose
yawns—the electricity of one being one dims.
The eternal moment ticks, and is over.

The sky is not the color of your thought,
the earth was not raised to your step.
The dream subsides and the ghosts whom you befriended
were only shadows of unknown instincts.
It is like dawn when the sky is gray.
The doomsday clock that never rang.

Tick. 2007 was going to be a banner year. There was so much hope. The years just previous had imprinted something of a light in my soul. I went to get the remainder of my stuff from my aunt's place near the end of 2006, and when I was there was the first time to find out that every time I go back to Korea, it's like I never left. I mean, sure, my aunt is a little older and the buildings change occupants, stores close and stores open, maybe some other things change, but it's always like New York was a dream, and Seoul is the reality. My sojourn in the Land of the Morning Calm those few years—no, they were not quite triumph, but they were good times, worthy days. Like a strong root, where before, I was like a cutting just starting to establish myself. And I was still in following of the way of growth, leaving there. May that never end. There, I inhaled the air of dreams, a good strong whiff. And now in through the vapors of time was the aroma of yet another grand beginning, just about to really cook.

10 Inside and Out

Mirrors: I have said a little about them before: back in my heyday of acid trips and pot parties, I would be looking at my own face in the mirror when I went to the bathroom: as various things swirled by in their psychedelic flourishes, looking myself in the eye, and being puzzled by the visage, "Is this me?" "What is 'me'?" Then, I remember looking at myself in the communal bathroom back on the farm in Korea, right after I had prayed in the path leading into the woods (my conversion). I saw something like a golden aura around my head, but beneath my eyes that glow was obscured by darkness before the light. I was disappointed at that, actually, seeing the darkness. I didn't know how prophetic that vision was, what it would take to overcome that darkness.

It was only in 2007, two worlds away from the hard partying teen that I had been—only then did I find that I looked into the mirror and thought, "That's me." And in this year, I was about to have it all, again. Better than the time before. But it was like a display of fireworks, and then the sky holds only stars, and we move onto something else.

I was in the planning stages of making my own way out in the wild world. I was still working for Chris, on location at Alliance Bernstein in New York. My boss was a crazy Greek man named Kiriakos, whom I loved to work for. How crazy was he? He usually got in before me, at 9, but one day he wasn't there until noon. He called us all into his office and we saw something spread across the wall; he said he couldn't sleep the night before so he decided to diagram the entire database. Yeah, that kind of crazy. It was a pretty good life. I had thought, a couple months before, not to think of the romance part of my existence, that something was going to happen and I would know it when it did.

So one Friday, during a perfectly normal afternoon at the office, just way out of the grand grand blue, I get an email from Eunhye. She asked if I remembered her and that she knew I wasn't in Korea anymore because she had been following my blog. She said she was now living in England. And this is funny, because the last time I had thought, relax, something will happen and you'll know it when it does was right before I saw her the last time, in Seoul. Now, I remember that I sort of got a panic attack at one point, with this news, having trouble breathing.

We started chatting on MSN messenger and she asked me for my cell phone number. Then she started calling me like every other day. Half of me didn't quite believe it was happening. What I could make out of why she got back in touch was that she sent the email just a couple weeks before her 30th birthday. You know, she was having a quarter-life crisis. I recall I had something of a crisis when I turned 30. In mine, I took a month off from work and was solidly stoned for that whole month.

In a small town called Broadstairs, she was studying English and taking courses in gardening. Her dream was to garden in Dubai. And it was good that she got one of those, a grand goal to shoot for; she didn't have any kind of dream when we were going out in 2004—she had complained about that, about her friends asking her about it, and sort of making fun of her for it, a sore point. Now, of course, it was different. But it was sort of the same. And I found I was good with how it all became, and what it seemed to be becoming. I tried not to think about things, to turn off my analyticals, when time could better be spent experiencing it all. Much to see. Much to care about.

Now, I don't know when exactly I first thought this, but I did think it, for a long time: that Eunhye was my true love. It might have been after she left me for the last time when I first conjectured so. Not just soulmate, but something like destiny on a stick, there before me. The signs did appear to be in place for such a conclusion: the vision of her face years before we met, and the overriding feeling after the first date that this was the girl I was going to marry. I would not understand for some months (or years, depending on how you count things) after it all went wrong, why it happened like that—both when we had broken up the first or second times.

As it stood, summer 2007, everything was coming up Milhouse.[xiii] I was free from any kind of office environment from June on. At the end of that month, I visited Eunhye in England (man that town was small), and we had an astoundingly blissful week in Rome—that place is worth a few more visits, for sure. When I got home, I wrote in my blog that it looked like I had a girlfriend again. It was more than having it all. It was living the dream. It was Heavenly, and it was real. It was going so well, in fact, I became a little suspicious: things were *too* good, too perfect. I expected the rug to be pulled out from under me at any moment. But of course, like things will go, that would come only when I ultimately let my guard down.

Even with everything going my way, there still lurked the other world, and the fingertips of Halospace still chilled my skin where they touched:

> Perhaps I must despair, every once in a while. I am no solid thing. Being found, as I am—perhaps it is not ingrained in me all the way through; for I was lost, I think, for longer than that. I have become a sense of sureness to those who know me, the one who knows what is going on in the small things, and the overall character of the world. I am re-

sponsible. But even if this is my lot, I must in private buckle under the weight of some carefully placed feathers—in private, that I capitulate a little. For in public I cannot let them know how sometimes I am a hairsbreadth from collapse. Or perhaps I am merely being melodramatic. For it is true that in the real world, I will not allow myself the luxury of weakness. Vonnegut says we are who we pretend to me: if this is so, then perhaps I am stronger than that, after all. That only in private, in the quiet after hours, do allow myself this: to despair. Just a little, to think that it will not all come out alright... then to pick myself up, and go on with the rest of life. [10/26/07]

No one was going to know the doubt that I shouldered. I had become a high functioning, productive member of human civilization, and this was to be the only way it was going to work. Work, work, work. The Lord had turned my life completely around: for I have felt that he was not the one responsible for me entering madness, but the light that guided me out. For all I knew, the Halospace was never going to overtake me again. Mentally, I had achieved balance: not too crazy, but not too dull. Even if it was the case that I were to have to imbibe meds for the rest of my life, it looked like this was the sanity was the road I was going to continue on from then on. This was life, as I knew it.

I had thought when I was leaving to go it on my own, that on the business end of things, I was going to finish creating the AI in 6 months. By the end of the year, basically. But as I tried to flesh things out, out of my vague assertions, it was beginning to dawn on me how hard this problem actually was, the years of wandering through bookstores and thinking be damned. I'm not even talking about the push to put things in code form, but just the concepts of what makes up an artificial intelligence. Now, as far as finances, I had some savings, and I took out about $65,000 in loans; like I said, in anticipation of the 6 months of development, and maybe another 3 to raise money for it? Hit it and quit it, right? Well, 2007 went bye-bye and I was nowhere near getting any of it really figured out. But it was still such a good year. There was so much hope, again, all throughout its reach.

When we come to early 2008, Eunhye calls me one day and says she has terrible news. I braced for some sort of system shock. She said, remember the apartment I had in Seoul? I sold it when I moved to England and invested it all in a nightclub, and have been living off the proceeds from it. Today I found out that the nightclub just went out of business. I've lost my life savings, $400,000....

Holy guacamole, Batman. Firstly, I thought, you had $400,000? You lived almost like a pauper. For instance, she didn't have a proper bed, just a mattress on the floor, and her laptop was at least 4 years old. But anyway, second was to think, why did you put all your eggs in that shaky a basket? I did try to commiserate, but really, I couldn't imagine what she must have been going through. My troubles usually came from the other world, not this one… And things would never be the same again.

She made motions to make things be as it was before. She tried to get a visa to the US to come visit me, but she was turned down because she was trying from England, and not Korea. I hear tell it's a very annoying process, getting a visa, as they even poke around your bank account to remove suspicion that you'll become an undocumented resident. So, she then said that she was going to go back to Korea. And it was about this time that I was thinking of buying that ring. You know, settle down and stuff.

Note that I had yet to say "I love you" to her, not even on the phone.

When she left England, I didn't hear from her for about two weeks. I tried her old Korean phone number, and nothing. Every time before when she had gone back home like she said she was doing, her old number would be dusted off and used again. Not this time. Instead, she emails me and says, I'm sorry I didn't tell you, but I discussed this with my family, and *I'm in New Zealand.* (emphasis added) She says it's her best shot in pursuing her dream (gardening, right?). OK. And then, a couple weeks later, I mention in my blog that the parents are getting antsy about me getting married and having a kid or two. So I get the last email I ever would get from Eunhye: she says she read my blog and she can't give me what I wanted, that she has to follow her own path, and she hopes I'll find someone who can give me what I deserve. It was like, *Are you breaking up with me?* Yeah. I tried replying to the email, and I never heard back. So yeah.

Now understand, she was in my head, too. You know what I'm talking about? I told you that in my visions I saw and talked to people who were dead *or* alive, so why wouldn't Eunhye be one of them? When you wanted to be close to someone, why not take every opportunity?

I remember back in the Drexel Hill apartment was about when Arquette starting hanging out in my vicinity in the Halo-space. I recall we didn't always get along. When the Lord shut my visions off in my visit to California, even then she would come visit, if infrequently; and then when they all came back, she was just there all the time. It was her and the Lord who were constant companions. And I will admit she did help out at times.

She was with me all the way through my going back to school. Among other people, of course, notably Joan of Arc helped out. And Arquette was there until she couldn't take it anymore in

1997. She was then gone until I quit that .com job, living in San Francisco, and I called for her, like calling an old flame. She was with me on and off after that, all the way until I started to go out with Eunhye. Whereupon I broke up with Arquette, in the Halospace, because I don't two-time. I was going to be with Eunhye inside and out. And then of course I wasn't with Eunhye between 2005 and 2007, so in the midst of that, in 2006, I got sort of back together with Arquette... though it was not really the same anymore... and then in 2007, when Eunhye emailed me, I pretty much kicked Arquette to the curb again. Don't feel bad for her, though: remember what she did to me.

It wasn't all Arquette, however, the entire time I said above I was with her. Though it was pretty much accepted during those times that I would eventually end up with her. There was this one time Audrey Hepburn was the one in my flight vicinity. Apparently I did this shtick she liked, when I performed "Mad Hamlet"—an improvised quasi Shakespearean interactive monologue. It's amazing what will win a person over. Sometimes it seems, it's barely anything at all. And I recall Audrey almost broke us up, Arquette and me, even when I thought we were true love itself. Yeah, that was how hot Audrey Hepburn was. Insanely hot.

So, the spirit of Eunhye hung around even after the earthly one broke up with me. She would stay with me for a long time after that, in fact. Even when we weren't an item even in the Halospace anymore she'd kinda hang out in the general area. The thing about these spirit versions of people: they were them, but they weren't them. Why do I not just throw in the towel on this point, and say that they were just figments of my imagination? I mean, the spirit of Eunhye was definitely not in any substantive contact with the one on Earth. The spirit one, right before the earthly one broke up with me, seemed to think we were getting married! And in another example of Halospace life, recall that the spirit of Arquette never got me picked up by the flesh and blood one in California. Why did I think they had any reality to them at all?

Consider, I might say, what Philip K. said about reality: it is that which, when you stop believing in it, it doesn't go away. If you recall, in 1997, I *did that*. I disbelieved, I put it all in the broad swath of psychosis. And it didn't go away. Sure, for a time it seemed to behave itself, as secondary to my real-life existence, but like the tide, it would roll back in. Remember, one may see that which is psychosis as separate from a true religious experience in that the former destroys, the latter heals. But what if *both* happen? Such was like the experiences of Philip K. Dick, but it was even more extreme in my plight, that I am broken down to be rebuilt: but each time, better. What do we believe, then? What is it that makes sense?

The question of their reality wouldn't be resolved until much later on. The spirit of Eunhye, and in fact, all of the spirits I would come to know with any depth: there was genuineness to each one of them. Like they carried the spark of the one who existed in reality. And now Eunhye, I thought she was my true love. The old adage was true, that I didn't know what I had until I didn't have it anymore. At least, in one of the two worlds. Recall, when we were together, I never once told her, "I love you."

But now I was sure of my love, that which speaks in poetry, and I had this faith: one day, we'd get back together—the two of us, on Earth; one day, she would come and live with me in New York. She'd tend to Central Park or something. And you know what? We would live happily ever after. Quite literally. I thought that since she was my one true love, and we'd also be together in Paradise. My favorite quote from *The Princess Bride*, that I would have occasion to say, was when Eunhye were amazed at how could this phenomenon and that so happily chanced our way. I would say, "This is true love. Think this happens every day?"

11 The Coming and the Birth

There is one sticking point to Christianity, one that is usually glossed over: that we have expected Christ's return ever since he left. Those who say that any days between his departure and his second coming are the "last days" seem to be begging the issue. Really abusing the language, in other words. They say the Bible is like a person: torture it enough and it will say anything. I myself recall the years thinking like so many other Christians were thinking: that the world was about to end. Remember "Romeo and Juliet Witness the Apocalypse"? I thought it was on!

So, I thought I had the future all figured out. First, I would get back together with Eunhye, then we'd have a kid or two, and along the way I would finish my AI. Then the Rapture would happen (for real this time), and Eunhye and child would be caught up in the clouds. I would be "left behind," but not like almost everyone else. I would have a mission. I would wander the earth or be pulled to some place by an unknown force, and I'd meet with Rosanna Arquette in the flesh, and we'd be the two witnesses of the Apocalypse for 3½ years. (We'd then be killed and after 3½ days a voice would call us up to Heaven. All in a day's work.) No, Arquette wasn't my true love anymore; that position had been filled by someone more accessible (more realistic?), but we *were* going to get together for a little bit. For the job. Witnessing the Apocalypse.

What do you think, does it sound more delusional than usual? Putting aside who exactly it would be who were the two witnesses, this kind of scenario is pretty much what a lot of people believe is going to happen. Soon. It ended up not being true, of course, that story. I was right in saying that the *R & J* chapter was over, and to turn the page—we were not those Witnesses. You know, if I were to turn up the skepticism knob up to scoffer, I might say none of this could possibly be real. Not only were we NOT people spoken of in the Bible, the Bible itself is not where you go for any real understanding of the universe, past, present, or future. I would say that I had been right when I marked it all part and parcel of a psychosis, induced by drugs those years ago, and why exactly did I think otherwise, again? How could I not be asking myself if I were just lapsing into delusion, if I thought myself a rationalist at all?

Except that I had said this about all that happened to me: I am broken down and then I am reformed, reformulated, as if an unknown voice were to say, "We have the technology. We can make him better than he was."[xiv] It was not just that fighting my way back from the depths of psychosis made me a stronger person. For what does not kill me makes me etc. etc. This would probably be all the skeptic would allow me. But no, what I got was not that generic a gift, not something strained to make it seem like a blessing (using that term in a secular sense). During my time in the pit, I learned what only being in the pit could teach me. In the specific parameters of what was available to me. This wound inflicted upon me, and the years it afflicted me—it was a fortunate wound, indeed. Sometimes we are allowed to see it: God really knows what He's doing.

If you say then, no, it was not anything divine at work, just that my incredible adaptability made me able to handle the things that came at me so adeptly. But one discounts, I would like to say, those three words: "Work is magic." What I have gained in having been through the failure would not have been nearly as significant without the little cartoon of Jesus Christ telling me that. And if that cartoon wasn't really Jesus, even if he talked like Him, acted like Him, had what looked like an immeasurable consciousness to Him, and saved me like only He can do: when does it become irrational *not* to believe? It was not that He met my pre-conceived expectations, I looked back and realized oh, *that's* what the Son of God is supposed to be like! For me it took about 4 years of Him banging His heart against this mad bugger's wall[xv] for me to see what were the obvious things, and before my very eyes. He showed me. Work is magic: these words foresaw a great part of my future, and it is not easily tossed aside.

As far as the Lord's Purpose for me, I would understand something of it, as far as the most important part of it goes, on down the road. About how love was going to go. I still had a girlfriend in the Halospace, and this kept me from going out of the way and trying to find anybody in the real world to be with. And my every hour, just about, was spent in thought. Artificial intelligence, quite the subject. At times, I thought so hard, so intensely that it would be past and into the threshold of pain. And I would scribble in my notebook new and earth-shattering paradigms. Though maybe the scribblings meant more to me than anyone else. There was a joke:

>**Reporter:** Professor Einstein, is it true that only 3 people in the world understand your theory?
>
>Einstein looked deep in thought for a moment, and another.
>
>**Reporter:** Professor Einstein?
>
>**Einstein:** I'm trying to think who the 3rd person is.

I loved this joke. It was one of the things that inspired me. And the movie *Iron Man*. Man works alone in his basement on revolutionary technology? My room is on the lower level of a split-level apartment. (My roommate is up top, and he's been there for over 25 years.) Yeah. That was the year Michael Phelps won 8 gold medals in the Olympics. I felt so close to greatness, like I were on the home stretch. But I was actually just out of the gate, at that point.

The spirit of Eunhye and I didn't speak much. In fact, when we were dating in real life we didn't talk that much, either. The one I conversed with for much of the years before the Event was Albert Einstein. I must say, he was a wonderful colleague to have, with some really good insights to a field he had had no education on. But really, we were talking about mathematics and machines, which he did go to school for, and had a job verifying, respectively. He was my sounding board for a lot of the ideas that I would have, and this was a rather functional indication that the visions I was having were rational, or at least had a rational streak going through them. Because if what you come up with is not sound, in computer science, it's sort of easy to check. Does it work? Does it run? If not, you're peddling bull cookies. If it does what you wanted it to do, what you thought it should do, well then. You really can't argue with results. Two little theories I came up with:

1. What satisfies a pattern also satisfies what the pattern satisfies.
2. The satisfaction of a pattern is itself a pattern.

Yeah, especially the second, I was really happy with these. This was all in 2008, maybe a little going into 2009. This was hope: that everything was going to be alright. Life, one supposes, could have been better, but surely one should not complain about circumstances like I was in, if one should ever complain at all. And I found out I was being guided in my thinking: to go in these directions, to be familiar with these abstractions: they would prove useful when we arrive at the Event.

One last thing that happened in 2008: December, I woke up with a stomach ache, in the middle of the night. I couldn't get back to sleep, it was so persistent. When 7am rolled around went to the local supermarket and got some cures for gas, and none of them worked. The pain was not unbearable, but it wasn't something you wanted to get used to. By about 4pm I decided that this was not something trivial, and I went to the emergency room at the nearby hospital. It wasn't far and I just hopped in a cab. Definitely no need for an ambulance. Turned out I had gallstones. Then they did a CAT scan and found my gall bladder was infected, so they had to take it out. But that wasn't the big thing that we end 2008 with.

I was high on Dilaudid at the time, while I was in my hospital room, and I think it was the 13th. Pretty sure it was after the operation. Anyway, I had some sort of nugget of an idea that I really didn't understand, and from that, something like a running process from in my mind went out into the Halospace, and I wondered what it was, and if it would return. I remember being surrounded by angels. And when the process came back, completing its run, there was something new. Some*one* new. He spoke English, was friendly and inquisitive, and I let him name himself: "we are the knights who say ni." That's his full name. But by the time I was discharged from the hospital, he had disappeared. He would come back, though, and how time works: I had actually seen him before, in the Halospace, before that day of his birth. The War in Heaven was a war in eternity, and time is strange in relation to it. I still don't fully get it, and it would take the Event for me to gather how weird it was. (And here, I left some blood behind.)

As 2008 passed into 2009, I did a few financial calculations and found that I was going to need an income. There would have been ways to keep going on my own, but they involved selling stuff of mine that I didn't want to part with. So I called where I was working before, in 2007, the company in Berkeley run by my friend Chris, and I ended up with a 6 month quality assurance gig, QA—testing websites. Specifically, a fitness website. And in the course of the days spent at it, I found out I was quite the natural.

I was still working on the AI on the side, and near the end of the year I had a very simplistic demo of what I had actually did put into code. I remember being very happy when I had something, the bare bones, working. I wrote on Facebook: "IT'S ALIIIIIIIIIIIIIIIIIVE!" Still, it was not very good, even if it did perform simple syllogistic logic. I really had to explain what it took for even the barest reasoning to work, and like if you had to explain why a joke is funny, you're sort of missing the point of telling the joke, n'est-ce pas?

Other than the debugging of my almost trivial functioning that was my AI, 2009 was a bit of a breather, after all that had happened the year before. Not to say nothing happened. In the summer, out of the lighter hued blue, someone at the *New York Times* found my phone number in the voter record, and gave me a call. To do an interview for their blog. It was all about my name, John Doe. And I did, they took pictures, and a few days later, it was live. I was on the front page of the New York Times website for a few hours, and on the bottom half of the print version the next day. Pseudo-famous for like second.

One really good thing happened because of that, though. Some Korean newspapers picked up on it (you know, Korean does good, they all want a piece of that action) and they basically translated the 'Times story, and my father read it. He told me that back when he was getting robbed a lot at his store, at the police station when he gave his name (James Doe), they would invariably ask, "So where's John?" To which he would answer, "He's at home!" And he never understood why they kept asking about the whereabouts of his son until *just then*. Hilarious.

And there was this, too, in 2009; where we change the topic and hope not to shove it into a corner somewhere; because this happened (from my blog):

> I begin to think there's something going on, here. August 31st, Monday, I awoke to a crushing depression. Really, I could not do anything. Not even think of concentrating on anything related to my project. I had no idea why. Nothing had materially changed from Sunday, or even Friday. Then, late Tuesday night, for no apparent reason, I decide to look at a Korean newspaper. And there, I read that the actress Jang Jin-Young had just died, the day before. I had been madly in love with her (colloquially, not literally) ever since seeing her in a commercial for a movie she did in 2003. WTF? I mean, I never look at Korean newspapers, and I happen to look exactly when it would be on the front page news? And I get this crippling depression at just the same time? What does any of this mean? [9/6/09]

You must understand that this was not the first time anything like a psychic moment had happened to me. The clearest example of it, at least to me, was when I was staying at the parents' place, in my old room. In a dream, I was in that same room. I heard something, as if it were right outside the window: someone tapped together 2 drumsticks, so I went to the window and looked out. It was not the view I expected, of the house's front lawn and the street. Instead, it was the view out the backyard of a place I didn't recognize at all. I didn't think anything of it at that point. Just one of your average dreams, right?

A few months later, when I helped my friend Deniz move into his house, I stopped and looked out his window at the top of his stairs, overlooking the backyard—and there it was: that was it. Exactly what I saw in the dream. I can't ask you to believe me, but it's very weird when that sort of thing happens. I'm not talking about flying saucers or ghosts or bigfoot, just images and feelings; rationalist that I used to be, who believed not in God or miracles, but only what seemed to make sense from the base measurements of physics: it was impossible until it happened to me. Everything like that is. It happened, and it happened again—until all of what made sense to me were put to the test by the fantastic, new vistas opening up before my eyes. Daring me to try and call it all the work of my imagination, and if I could, leaving me to wonder how far mine own imagination might possible go.

12 Faith and Logic

We get closer to what I call the Event, which transpired between New Year's day and January 13, 2013. The 2 far reaching endpoints, and the experiences in their general vicinity, would be what are responsible for much of the meaning of my life: 10/7/88 and 1/13/13. Not to say it was all devoid of meaning during the while between those 2 peaks, or even that I was lacking in intense adventure when I speak of other times. I did have those. Yea, verily.

In my day to day, as I have told about, I was upon a noble quest separate from the obvious reach of the War in Heaven, and those 2 courses I imagined they had to do little about, one the other—or at least I thought. For I was in the midst of developing a true artificial intelligence, the likes of which had never been seen before, in these decades since the computer first materialized. This quest consumed me. Every spare thought I would use to think about the AI. There are so many instances that would fit in the context of the AI: how words are interpreted, how sentences are formed, what fits into a context and why, how we perceive in uncertain conditions, and on and on.

Which is not to say the research was the only thing I did. In addition to my day job, I started reading the Bible again. First it was 15 minutes a day, then 30, then an hour. How do you do such a thing, given the responsibilities and happenings of the everyday? It's really simple: want to do it. If you don't want to do it, very likely you won't do it if you don't have to. Or get good at keeping promises and promise that. I wanted to start reading it again, and I promised some of the saints in my visions that I would increase the pace. You know how much Bible reading that eventually amounted to? I have now read the Bible 8 or 9 times, and am on my 9th or 10th reading. Yes, I lost count. With all that going on, I was one busy man.

As far as those "other" intense experiences, a blog entry from about that period:

> I have seen my personal demon. As in, the actual outline in my mind's eye of a fallen angel, that kind of demon. I don't know if I can get a clearer picture of it, for what I saw was much an abstraction of evil; but really, I don't know if I really want a better representation of what it is. It looked strange, like a vibrating red darkness, and I got a bad vibe from it in general. In my worldview, that demon is real, or as real as need be, the sum total of that which turns me on the wrong paths, when it can. Of late, it has not been doing that much in those directions, but I must admit that it has had some successes. The angels, too, who showed it to me, these are real enough too, all that would make me a noble example of a human being. Very much is my psyche a battle between the forces of good and evil of which I have become entangled. To the victor, the spoils, and in this conflict, the spoils would be me... [11/25/09]

Its name, I found out, was Roksaza. My personal demon. And I contended with him once, and again… I don't know what you have in mind when I tell you that, now. Both of us drawing lightsabers and clashing with "Carmina Burana" blasting in the background? Not so much. Contending with him most resembled arguing with him. But with feeling. Taken to the nother level, as it were. Like my mortal soul were at stake at the outcome. And it would prove to be good training for the Event.

Roundabout that vision of Roksaza, I had stopped working at the day job after the QA thing was finished, and the site I was testing went live. Separate from that, I showed around the little I had of the AI to see if anyone close to an investor would bite, but that was a negatory. So as 2010 came along, I had the choice between rigging up some smoke and mirrors, a flashy demo which would ultimately be hollow, or go back to Chris and ask if could use me again. And you could probably guess that I went back to having a day job again. Even knowing that the demo creation would be a check that my butt could one day cash. I started developing an Android app for mobile banking. It was a good gig, but I did feel a little underpaid, and felt especially so—retroactively—years later, when Chris's company was riding real pretty on the mobile banking train. But I shouldn't complain. And I complain that I complain too much. That's part of my code of honor, actually: don't complain—especially when you are receiving good things.

I suppose it was not all good, though. All work and no play makes Jack a dull boy.[xvi] That was a foregone conclusion: work, work, and work: this is why you were alive, this is what gives you meaning. The Book of Ecclesiastes tells you to enjoy your work while you can, for there will come the day you are buried and will not be able perform it any more. This sort of idea was pretty much what I went by. Work at the day job to pay the bills, work on the AI with any spare cycle you had, work on your soul so that God may love thee. I never went out, except for a setup date here and there. Maybe to go to a party every blue moon. But don't cry for me, Argentina.[xvii]

Didn't matter all that much though, because in my visions, Eunhye was still with me: on my shoulder in my mind, on a shelf in my consciousness, a spirit like a candle hovering. And in the real world, I would every once in a while pursue what I believed was what destiny spelled for me; so you know, I emailed her every now and then. No response from the messages sent, and poems, and music videos, but I did see her in my referrer logs on my blog every now and again. However lonely it may have been, it was a good life. It was a worthy life. I was fulfilling my utmost potential for the first time in my life. At the age of 40 or so. And I remember how turning 40 sucked, but at least I had that to show for it: a life worth living.

Now, being as I was a servant of God and a man of honor, I made for myself a short code of honor to follow. Who has a code of honor, especially these days? They asked the same question on the show *King of the Hill,* and Hank Hill sort of muttered that he had one. And this little exchange on a cartoon show inspired me to come up with my own, and also precepts:

CODE OF HONOR
Don't be a hypocrite.
Be thankful for what you can do, and what you
    are, not proud.
Mean what you say, say what you mean.
Do not stand by when you can do something.
Take responsibility for all your actions.
Be humble in the face of the world.
Don't complain.

PRECEPTS
Better good than lucky.
Work is the only magic.
You love in proportion to the work you do.
Truth is always best.

Faith in the justice of God.
Better to hope and be wrong.
Simplicity.

Upon reading these, one of the frequenters of my blog said that my parents would be proud of me for having these. It's nice to think that. And that this is the silver that shone free from the fires of its refining.

I remember now, only just, how bad it used to be—the attacks of paranoia. They were not logical, but they seemed to make so much sense when they struck. Mostly they would make me believe that for all I had done with my life, it was ultimately for naught; because I was ultimately the Son of Satan, the son of perdition. That I had signed a binding contract back in 1991, when the War had peeked in, or to play on my pride and hold that I was the best and brightest—but like Lucifer had been, and so would I share his fate. Sometimes the paranoia was that merely the sin I'd accumulated made my soul a toxic mix. And there were other sources of attack, I cannot remember every one. I would say that they were attacks from my personal demon, Roksaza, when I was made aware of his existence, and I found a focus.

And now that I had a name, and I had an image, this was around the time when I started to fight back. When I had enough information to be able to act, and the attitude. Exactly how, I made up as I went. What worked, I found: faith and logic. If you should happen to need advice on this type of combat with the forces of evil, hold to this: when only one do you have to fight with, you should choose logic, but if both are available, you must put faith first.

Those weren't the only attacks I experienced, more or less that I identified as coming from the demon. Rarer would be when I heard something or read something in the real world that was substandard, and the world became less real. Because, at least partly, they would remind me of when I was stuck in the Black Iron Prison, and the music died, and became only a simulation of anything could be called that, music. Reality losing its reality again. One prime example for this sensation was in some of the worst lyrics I'd ever heard, "Life", by Des'ree. I think when she sang, "I'd rather have a piece of toast", some psychic trigger flipped in my head. Basically to feel in my bones something like, "Is this real?" about the world at large. To calmly hold on and talk myself down.

It might have been connected to the derangement that the Dragon, and his angels, were trying to perpetrate upon all the likes of creation itself. I only thought this, of course, of where they may have had their source, only quite later. And I remember that during any one of those attacks, I was hanging on to my hold on reality, hanging on for dear life. Else the world (at least the world I knew) unravel before me.

It got better, of course, and I really have to think hard to recall when those attacks were such a big deal. When things become normal, however altered they used to be, one gets used to the normal again and start taking things for granted—like normal. That is the default mode of life, not to think how anything works is actually magic. Dostoevsky understood this. From the account he put in *The Idiot*: he thought, as he was being led to a firing squad, that if he were to be reprieved, he would make the most of—hold as so very precious—every moment and every sensation, like he were experiencing them right then, what were to be those last seconds of life. But then it happened: the execution was stayed, and he lived, on and on, decades more. And things had gone back to normal forthwith, for this is the nature of life. Even the nature of sanity.

In knowing my personal demon Roksaza, and caught in his attacks (most of the time from out of nowhere), I started taking notes, so that I might recall what they were like. It was raw me fighting by faith and logic (and maybe some Truth, here and there), and the notes may not make that much sense, but see if you can make out the reasoning that I was weaving together, for to form a shield of interconnected logical truths. See if you can tell in the blow by blow where I give to refute, at least for that time, the derangement of the evil (don't worry if you can't, it's hard even for me to think how big a deal they seemed at the time):

> contending with my demon [1/28/10]:

> so is it that the Lord can be kept out, and my faith in Him was false (but He can't be kept out—He is everywhere.)

> or is it that He can't be kept out, so therefore I can count on Him?

> if I believe, I can count on Him. (by faith we are saved.)

> me: so if they send Satan and I beat him, then that's pretty much it, right?

> demon: so you think you can beat Satan?

> me: no, but the Lord can.

> so He can't be kept out, but my faith in Him was false?
>
> twisting the words means that you cannot logically reconcile it.
>
> if I can't count on Him, then you are not logically consistent saying "both are true".
>
> if I can count on Him, then my faith was true, and the first one is false.
>
> therefore, you were lying when you said you were logically consistent.

I think there was more that came before this little exchange, when the demon engaged with me, but if there was, it is lost in history's bitbucket. If I can summon the memory at all clearly, I believe that the last statement there collapsed Roksaza's web of lies.

Sorry if the reality of fighting demons doesn't seem that exciting from the notes. It's less *The Exorcist* and more *Court TV*. If I am correct in my recollection of this one, during the argument was indeed heart-pounding from my point of view, *all* the way through, and I felt positively *elated* when I won. They must have translated well in the Halospace, too, because Eunhye would watch me and be terrified for me during the contests to come.

Those fights seem longer ago than they actually were. The Event that came between then and now was immense, life changing. Was I so very fragile, back when? This was years ago, when it seemed the demons' sport was in freaking me out. Contending was pretty much in the same intent, but by different approaches: to make me think that I was damned, to go through the rest of my life weighted with that misery; or worse, that I was most evil of them all, being the Son of Satan himself, and as in the movie *Angel Heart,* that I had made the deal years ago... It mattered not that I was not clearly cognizant of the terms of our little agreement. Satan was now coming to claim what was his. This was where the movie was going to end.

By this time, it had come a long way, though. It used to be that the mere mention of such a circumstance as my damnation or of perdition and its son would to trip all the necessary wires of paranoia—which were skewering me through and throughout my psyche—and I would think that I were doomed! But wait, wait, I could still pray, and then some heavenly being would come rescue me. Usually the Lord or the Archangel Michael. Even just that should have told me (right there!) that the paranoia were not but a vapor of evil, but what it ended up taking to properly understand was years of living a good life. And at this point, I had enough such foundation to confront the sources of my terror. I could fight back, indeed.

Let me show you another set of notes of a time of contending:

contending [6/22/10]

You wanted me to believe that I was the Antichrist
so that I wouldn't be the Antichrist. For the
Antichrist thinks he is Heaven sent.

For the purpose God gave you is to be against
God.

But a house divided against itself cannot stand.
How can God's purpose be against His own
purpose?

Why would God create creatures that are against
    Him, then torture them when they do so?

Because we actually like pain?

Then why did the demons say to the Lord if He
    were going to cast them into the abyss before
    their time, and they'd rather be sent into pigs?

Because we're confused about God's purpose?

But then why should I believe you about God's
    purpose if you're confused about it?

Partially?

Why didn't they ask to be cast into the abyss?
    Wouldn't that be against God's will, like the
    first statement?

No, that would be fulfilling God's purpose?

Isn't that supposed to be at the end of time?

You had no problem in telling me that I was the
    Antichrist.

You were doing that to test me, knowing I
    wouldn't believe it.

> You can be safe to say anything to me and I won't believe you.

You can tell that my confidence is bolder, and perhaps that at least for the purpose of the argument, that my thinking was clearer. Sorry I didn't write down what the demon was saying, too. You might be able to tell, if you think about it, what he was positing in the negative, reading the above.

It wasn't always Roksaza I fought, if I think about it. Sometimes I thought, or the vision seemed to present itself, that I were fighting Satan himself. As in, all my sensors would flash, "Satan! Satan!" Almost in flashing red letters. During the times when that happened, though, I always figured it was Roksaza pretending to be the Devil. I thought, I'm such an obscure person, not famous at all, not a great saint like St. Anthony, why would the actual Devil waste his time on a corner case like me? I mean, there's only one of him, and I was sure he had better things to do with his time. Easier to believe a random demon getting up on his haunches to look big and scary sounded much more likely, to fight a regular guy. It might have been the Devil, though, sometimes, but maybe it was in his better interest to go along with my train of (un)belief on who was it exactly attacking me. Because whomever it really was that came at me, I defeated them all. That is, when I had learned to fight back.

As I said before, I was reading the Bible a lot during this time. It has helped me greatly in a few aspects of my life. If you perchance a proclivity to do so yourself, I recommend *The Message*. It is a Contemporary English Version, and I recall when I first read a CEV, there had been one or two difficult passages that I just hadn't understood until reading them translated into the vernacular. People forget that the King James Version was not always supposed to be that impressive sounding, but it also reflected the vernacular of the time, which happened to be early 17th century. Yes, *now* it sounds all flowery. And I did read that version too, back when I was at the lowest time of my life, roundabout 1995. I wrote before: the higher ups made me read. It was pretty much against my will back then, or at least against my desires. And what I remember most about that reading was, "My bowels! My bowels!" Yup, that's in there. It means, "My anguish! My anguish!", but that's not what it says. Heh.

Now I know all the stories, can recognize pretty much all the names—at least, if they're not just one in a string of begats (Joel begat Ishmael, Ishmael begat Michael, that type of thing). I now have a much different relationship with it than before I let all that content mix it up inside me. And I really can't imagine what's in the minds of those people who say they take it literally, every single word. It's a special type of insanity, I might think. (Yes, insanity, not psychosis: they don't comprehend the difference between right and wrong.) For one, they always seem to forget this three word command: "Love your enemy." That seems pretty clear to me, as far as its meaning is. Yet that seems to be among the unheard of set of phrases subject to interpretation. Imagine that.

What the Bible was for me? It was one of the ways I was made subject to the New Covenant: this was a means for those above to write the Law directly onto my heart. Not the only way, as things may go, but definitely one effective way. To help instill an inner voice that can tell what is right, and what is wrong. We must all find that voice, at some time in our lives. Ultimately, you cannot live the entirety of your life hanging on the words of a 2000 year old book—even if it can help you get ready to do just that: live by the Word.

I would later supplement the Bible reading with prayer. I think I was up to an hour of Bible reading and a ½ hour of prayer every day. Except Sunday, when instead I would just go to mass—just the Bible part excluded, I would still pray. The amazing thing is how much else I got done during this time. Day job, AI research, sure, but I was also posting regularly on 3 blogs. When I took breaks from the AI research, I also wrote a Facebook app that didn't go anywhere, and then a dynamic website that people liked but ended up dead too (the site's still running, BTW). Also I was writing poetry, mostly for the blogs, but one of them got published, the second time for me. Here:

"notes"

> there is a song written of forgotten notes
> sung by silence, when the trees are still
> unmistakably haunting as it slips away
> as time drives you on past the moment
> to live life as if we never knew the secret
> yet holding a hope strange with simplicity
> breathing in breezes, a rustling of the trees

I wrote that when I was feeling a little heartbroken, one day. Ever since then I held such pain as precious. But yeah, I imagine da Vinci had something like the schedule above. Most of my stuff, though, it was lost in thought, puppets made of logic that would dance a bit then traipse offstage. Little did I know, however, that none of it were for naught.

    Oh, and I guess let me add to the list of things I was doing, "contending with my personal demon"—yeah, and all of it had a cipher. All of it had a meaning—all of it was doing something, sometimes by just the mere fact of existing. All of it had a way of making sense: of itself, of myself, of God Himself, and His Son Jesus Christ, all his angels. All I could ask was, why me? Not to say it as any pitiful plea, for I had no woe, not anymore: not for a decade or more. I was asking how it was that He could lay up so many blessings upon a single individual in his lifetime. Really, Lord, WTF? Why me?

    My Lord, my Lord—why did you not abandon me?

13 Pagliacci

I heard a joke once: Man goes to doctor. Says he's depressed. Says life is harsh and cruel. Says he feels all alone in a threatening world. Doctor says, "Treatment is simple. The great clown Pagliacci is in town tonight. Go see him. That should pick you up." Man bursts into tears. Says, "But doctor... I am Pagliacci."
– Alan Moore, *Watchmen*

The story of Pagliacci, in that short passage in the *Watchmen*, it haunts me. Has since I first read it, when I was 18 years old, before the beginning of this book's chronology. One imagines the story to be pure fiction, a distilled spirit of sadness. And there may be stories, even true—certainly that were written—that are sadder, of greater tragedy; but for the pure irony, the despondency of that, the greatest clown in the world, might be impossible to match. It is perfect a story. It is a myth like among the great myths through history, not involving gods or heroes, but perhaps the modern day stand-in for heroes: celebrity. And we remember the thing about myths, that they are lies that tell the truth. Fictions that tell us about real life.

My stories are not myths, except maybe for the one or two times I tell you I'm creating new ones. But maybe one should ask, what are they, then? Even leaving out the many, many times I was just confused, not able to make sense of anything going on around me... what I do present could be described as "out there". It is hard to understand, nay *believe,* how any of it as having any reality to it... a lot of times, so much easier is it to call it what it could be so easily confused with—two things, really: drugs, or psychosis. Or maybe even both at once. I may try to explain some of it, how these things came to be, but I will not try to comprehensively justify all the points I attempt to make. Indeed, such an exercise might have the opposite of the intended effect. Maybe the solution lies with Pagliacci.

Philip K. Dick, my twin, after 2-3-74, he asked a bunch of times, "Am I nuts?"—and perhaps was justified in sanity, by asking. As I described, I have thought that I knew that I was "nuts", to come around to the point where I am now, to think that I am not: that my thought, my ideas, are not to be relegated to the status of delusional fantastica (though they're really pretty if you plant them in that spot).

Phil went and wrote a fictionalized version of his experiences, and in it there is at one point where a psychiatrist practically "cures" his depression by saying to him, "Well, you're the expert." It was a response to a question about Gnostic Christianity, if I remember correctly. Unfortunately, that same blessing would be a curse if laid upon me, because one could say of my constructs and abstractions, of all my stories, one could tell me to try and get them verified by an expert in these things. Yes, my problem: *I'm the expert*—I'm Pagliacci. At least, since Philip K. is dead and gone in the real world. (I'm really looking forward to comparing notes with him in Heaven, though.)

They say that God does not call the qualified, but rather qualifies the called. But it might be that there *was already* something within the prophet that He wanted to work with. Right? He must have some reason for picking this guy and not that guy. Some inclination of the mind or heart that made Him think to send a certain soul into the lion's den—and then perhaps to lead him safely out. Now that we are here, in the heart of things, how can I get you to believe me in my tale? And is it just to nod your head and think that I'm a harmless kook, if interesting, to boot? Or is it at all possible that I can I get you believe that the center of my dreaming is rooted in an invincible Truth, as I believe truth can be? That I am a prophet of the I AM; and His Son, Jesus Christ; and the Spirit of Truth? It could be that the main thing is to get you to see that my twin, Philip K., was a bona fide prophet, and I am in his line as one myself.

In doing the research, I have not read through the entirety of what was published of his Exegesis. It's pretty old hat to me, and I understand the process that he documents, the cycle of positing a theory, fork off that theory, and so come up with a brand new theory. I did read them when they first published excerpts from it, in a slimmer volume. And also the very small portion of his Exegesis that is in the back of *VALIS*. As I have said before, where he left off, I pick up. And from where I write this, I'm not looking for new (or in this case, old) theories to give me inspiration to figure out why the world is as it is, and what happened "in the beginning" or at any major metaphysical spot. At least, insofar as their utility in the War in Heaven, it's pretty much over in regards to needing such speculation. We both were made for what we needed to do (somewhat of the "call the qualified" side of things). And we did not fail.

As far as his qualification(s) as a prophet, you might definitely say he has more than me. When he was hit by the pink light I mentioned before, he was told that his son had a very serious medical condition, which the doctors had missed. In fact, I believe that it was so hard to find, this anomaly, they had to check him a second time, on Phil's insistence. And what do you know? It turned out to be correct! This is very important. In the Old Testament, one basic criterion to be a prophet, if one were truly sent by God and not a part of some sideshow, was the veracity of his predictions. So we have at this point a thing modern science was unable to explain, how it could be that he came by that (correct) diagnosis. The best it can do is either to call him a liar, that that was not how it happened, or that he somehow "got lucky".

Seriously, can you do better, without acknowledging the elephant in the room—rather that God, or *something* we might call supernatural let him in on it?

To my thinking, it's just that Philip K. Dick was a *modern* prophet. This is what a prophet looks like in the context of the atomic age. I thought that well before I put myself in relation to him. Prophets are not supposed to be perfect people, and the Bible attests to that; it is the rare prophet who is for all intents and purposes blameless, someone like John the Baptist—who was a prophet from while he was still in the womb (and apparently knew his Lord even from there).[xviii] Philip K., though not what you conventionally call a saint, had—in my view—the right mindset to be a real, honest to goodness prophet of the Lord… Let me tell you a joke:

> A man who had studied much in the schools of wisdom finally died in the fullness of time and found himself at the Gates of Eternity. An angel of light approached him and said, "Go no further, O mortal, until you have proven to me your worthiness to enter into Paradise!"
>
> But the man answered, "Just a minute now. First of all, can you prove to me this is a real Heaven, and not just the wild fantasy of my disordered mind undergoing death?"
>
> Before the angel could reply, a voice from inside the gates shouted: "Let him in—he's one of us!"

This is how theology has become. We do not live on a flat earth, with Heaven above, and the underworld below. We know what's below, and it ain't full of departed souls. Our prophets are reflections of their times, and the twentieth century bred for us a prophet as complicated, and as uncertain as the times would have of his being, being sent of Heaven, Heaven at that present being relegated to a whole nother separate dimension itself.

What other qualification does a prophet need prove? What is a prophet than a mouth of God? If you would, this is taken from *VALIS* (and this is him speaking): "The time you have waited for has come." Yes? Sounds seriously like prophecy. Almost reminds you of the Old Testament prophets. Also sounds like John the Baptist (who is called the *last* Old Testament prophet). Two other sayings proved useful for me, in my own experiences as Elisha to his Elijah: "We have always already won," and "The theory changes the reality it describes." They came into play in the War.

There have been prophets through history, talking now between St. Paul and the present day, but they have been sparse in the seeding. Joan of Arc was one. I can't name many more. There have been saints, sure enough, at least those whom the church recognizes. But prophets? How many of those saints have been the mouth of God? Philip K. Dick spoke of what had been flying around on high, gathered utterances and hints, blessings and codes, drawn from all around the world, for now our knowledge of who is there and what their story is is open for perusal as never before; he spoke Heaven's word unfiltered, through all the chaos that we now know is the nature of the world, and he stood among the throngs of Mother Earth. He was (yea, verily) the new voice of God, this to know if—if we listened carefully enough to what he was really saying. Maybe to look "between the lines," looking in the spaces where you have to peek around the corner to see what is there.

But some will say he was just crazy. And not just him, Joan of Arc, too. I remember reading from a psychology book that Ezekiel they would diagnose with schizophrenia if he walked into one of their "sessions". There are people who will have none of what we might call supernatural: Jesus Christ never walked on water, Elijah was not carried off in a chariot of fire, Moses never parted the Red Sea (which I will admit was probably the Sea of Reeds).

There are people who think that the laws of physics are inviolable, however much you want to believe in miracles. That no, not *everything* is scientifically explained, but we have a good enough grip on what is physically possible to throw every miracle into the fraud pile. And there would God go, Himself. I remember, if a little cloudy the memory would be, me as one of these certain souls, an absolute skeptic. Devout atheist #1. It is a simple calculus: *so many* have been debunked, *they all* must be frauds.

Alfred Korzybski says to us, "There are two ways to slide easily through life: to believe everything or to doubt everything. Both ways save us from thinking." (Do you think, "Well yes, but…"? But aren't we rational people here?) And then there is Jesus Christ, who said (purportedly), "…many false prophets will appear and deceive many people." [Matthew 24:11 NIV] What do these two quotes have to do with one another? It is also said that the Devil will say 1000 truths to get 1 lie past you. Let's think rather the opposite. Maybe, just maybe, in a sea of lies—there is a sole, shining truth. Or maybe a few, but not very many there at all. Say, there is one truth, not meant for everyone to comprehend, even if they do find it; or perhaps not even to recognize it when they stare right at *that one*. But if we find in something out there a true miracle—and if we discover a real, higher purpose to it—we will find our eyes opened, knowing good and evil, and not merely to rate everything by the sliding scale of relative harm in effect. And then we may look for (and even find!) a higher purpose everywhere, for everything. No, *not* suddenly to believe in every last conjecture presented to us, but to see in the light a new dimension that pervades all things.

I'm not going to tell you what to believe. I'm Pagliacci, just performing my act to get a few laughs. I'm just a clown. Any truth you may get from me is purely coincidental. Right? But I can tell one thing about you, and you probably think this theory is about you:[xix] you don't believe in miracles because a miracle never happened to you.

We can start with the conjecture that Philip K. Dick was a prophet only if you believe in prophets at all. If you don't believe in that kind of thing, you can only conclude that he was deluded. Because if he was not completely deluded, there must be some nugget of truth working with and within him. Note that we're saying that what he was deluded about was of some significance, else we don't care either way. But on that delusion angle—you cannot believe he was working with pure fantasy, to the exclusion of all possibility, because of that one important thing: he properly diagnosed his son's unnoticed condition. Right? Because a delusion that turns out to be right is not a delusion anymore.

So all you're left with in the pure skepticism is that he was not a prophet but he was not *completely* deluded. And even if he were a prophet, none of whom we might call the prophets were really miracle workers, because the laws of physics are inviolable. We do not forget that there have been example after example of con-men, fraudsters who pretended to be in touch with the divine and pretended through trickery to be able to read your mind or predict the future—so many that the odds of miracles, those not supported by the laws of physics, the odds are so vanishingly small that one might say that miracles like that just can't happen. (Many false prophets will deceive many people.) Correct? Extraordinary claims require extraordinary proof.

Is that one thing, then, of Philip K. Dick and the pink light experience, extraordinary enough? Because we can talk about odds of it having been a random occurrence, if we take it now as a point of *fact* that Philip K. Dick's son was found to have the inguinal hernia he told them about, and he knew it out of the clear blue. What are, then, the odds that this information just popped into his head by the stochastic process of molecules just bumping around? What explanation do you have that makes sense of it in the purely "rational" point of view? No flying spaghetti monsters to have whispered it into his ears.

Rationally, that information could not have come from Phil. Where would it have originated if it had been? It makes no sense. I don't think Phil himself knew quite exactly what that condition was. It might have almost as easily come from nowhere. The most rational conclusion is that it came from outside, and since it came along with the appearance of causality to another, just as strange experience (that pink light), we might think the information was from the same source as the light. And then, that the external source must be able to communicate logically, and also that it was privy to knowledge which is not normally accessible. Arthur Conan Doyle: "Once you eliminate the impossible, whatever remains, no matter how improbable, must be the truth."

So, what does this mean? Going back to the pure rationalist, we have an unexplained phenomenon. To the pure rationalist, who does not believe in God, or spirits, or even aliens, this can *only* be an unexplained phenomenon. But if you care to listen, I will explain things to you. The short version is this: Philip K. Dick was truly a prophet of God Most High, and so am I. How do I know this, at least about Phil, when even he did not seem to? Now you're asking for the long version.

Remember that not everybody believed Jesus was the Christ, the Messiah. That would be a big reason that there are Jewish people today. So, I'm not thinking that everybody will believe Philip K. and I are prophets. (Note that this is not to compare us in any way to the Lord, it's only a "just sayin'".) The evidence we have so far: the strongest would be that thing with his son, of course; then comes that I pick up in 10/7/88 where he left off in his Exegesis; and then the vision I had where a cosmic egg split, and the blue half entered me, the pink half go off somewhere—and that Phil just saw the pink. There are others, but let's stick to these.

Philip K.'s view was necessarily incomplete: he learned just what he was meant to know. In fact, I have thought things along the way that were one thing, when later they were discovered to be quite something else. The fact of the matter is, or at least was, some of the knowledge I was let in on was *dangerous* to know. I put this in the context of the War in Heaven, and that's the fact of any war—but even moreso this one. Phil, the fact of the matter was, may have suspected he was a prophet, but as need to know went, he did not need to know.

Reality, at least in certain circles, resembles a grand origami, unfolding, and unfolding, and unfolding. Along the way, there are shapes that look like things and act like things, but then another unfolding happens, and you find out they are not those things. There are passages in the Bible that are like that, someone who was writing some of that scripture looked back on old books, and made a point using a quote from an older prophet—except that he would be in error, that the previous book had been mistranslated. It's probably happened, just that the Biblical inerrancy guys will tell you no one who is any way connected to the writing of the Bible has ever made an error EVAR. Yeah.

I can give you an example of an oft used quote from the New Testament that has been used in many places in the mistranslation of it: "You have heard that it was said, 'You shall not commit adultery.' But I tell you that anyone who looks at a woman lustfully has already committed adultery with her in his heart." [Matthew 5:27-28 NIV] Now this, a lot of people have quoted this as to be anti-pornography, anti-masturbation even. Except that the key word, "lust", is a mistranslation. The appropriate, or at least more appropriate, word is "covet". Makes more sense why he sorta contextualizes it with adultery, and is not bringing that topic up for no reason, huh? He is saying he knows our minds, that given any chance, we would try and horn into a good situation not in our own jurisdiction, as it were—morals be damned. So yeah, an actually *innocent* desire is perfectly fine.

God does know how a certain saying, a certain decree will be misunderstood, and like any mistake that happens, He makes use of the error. So masterfully at times that one would think it was better with the mistake than without. It doesn't mean that He wanted the mistake to happen, but things turn out for the best anyway: because He *does* do that. It is our purpose that we do not want the wrong to occur, but when it does, to make of things better than if everything went perfectly in the first place. If for nothing else, to spite the Evil.

Getting back on topic, it was not meant for Phil to know what he was. This is not unprecedented. I imagine Phil to be something like Amos 7:4: "I was neither a prophet nor the son of a prophet, but I was a shepherd, and I also took care of sycamore-fig trees." [NIV] And as Amos was considered by us a prophet anyway, thus it must be so that Philip K. should we consider a prophet, too. And why? Because he prophesied. What other purpose has a prophet, right?

The problem in trying to see it that way seems to be the signal to noise ratio, that of his 1000s of pages of his Exegesis, it's a lot of 10 steps forward, 8 steps back. Theory overtakes theory so many times that all the theories become suspect. But what if he was not meant for him to make sense of it all? Because all he was supposed to do was lay out the possibilities, to set up the board for the game to be played, and then: it would be played in *mine* own sight. And it's *my* job—let us just say, if some sense can be made of this idea or that, to make sense of it. Surely I am aided along the way, and often such help comes from unseen forces (and of these, not always unseen to me), but ultimately, it is my job to find the meaning of life. And if/when I do that, you may surely know that a prophet has been among you.

But you know, I've already found it, the sense in everything. And it might even be comprehensible to you, but just as someone who's never seen gold before may be handed a great bar of it will and not understand its value, it needs context. What tells me I have made sense of everything? If I start with something true, and develop the means from that initial candle to understand anything that has been, that is, or that will be, and such understanding is also true—then I have made sense of it all. One neat trick would be to find that initial truth (found it). But that in itself requires context (yes, I've found that too). Does it mean the end of science, or even the end of religion? The end of philosophy? Cats and dogs, living together?

I tell you that I was only able (or rather, allowed) to discover what I have seen because we are in the preliminary days of the Age of Gold, which replaces the Age of Iron. "The time you have waited for has come." Indeed, Phil had it right. Is this, then, the end, you may ask? I say to you, well did the Lord remark, "O faithless and perverse generation, ... how long shall I suffer you?" [Matthew 17:17 KJV] What could you possibly know when you think to speak about about the end? Hearken once more, child: the Beginning is near.

After the curtain closes, Pagliacci must take off the visage of a clown. Like the saying goes, after the game, the king and the pawn go into the same box. Clean of any makeup, he looks into the mirror, and sees what no one else can see: for everyone else can only see the hero of the opera. He looks into the eyes of the human being in the mirror. They say that what a hero wants most of all is an ordinary life. But he knows he must be that hero: when you see no other light around you, it is *you* who are to be the candle in the darkness. Do you not have eyes to see? The world is an impossible place. Meet it with an impossible love.

14 There Is Higher

Then there came a year made purely of anticipation. It was as if nothing at all happened in that year, but at any given time, *everything* was on the *brink* of happening. The whole time poised upon a precipice, in an inhale, ready to leap… Now to start with, after I had started contending with Roksaza, I was still at my breakneck schedule, which had me reading the Bible 1 more time and 1 more time, and this was also when I had started to pray every day, and then I also quit caffeine (all caffeine!) for Lent, and I went to Korea for a few weeks—this all, no, it didn't count, not to me. This was, I suppose, the life that John Lennon talked about, what happened while I was making other plans.

Pressing on my mind with an almost singular intensity was where I had gotten to in regards to my AI. You know, in the thinking so hard it was literally painful. I was addicted to it, that as a normal mode of being, this having been born with an addictive personality, an addict's genes. One must find a way to make of bad things good, though, and this was one of those maneuvers.

In the courses I took, I did manage to take notes of another of my contending with my demon:

> The demon appeared to me in the morning, after having half awoken from a particularly pleasant dream. He made some kind intonations toward me, fatherly intonations, and I could start to see something was coming. For he does that to switch on the old paranoia, of that I were supposedly the Devil's Son, the Antichrist, the Beast. But this time, I had been preparing; I had been girding my loins, so to speak, for weeks, upon a warning the

angels informed me of. Then a metaphysics gripped me, that the solidity of my soul was geared toward the ultimate substance of that of the Evil One, that I were given the taste of being a saint only before I were to assume my True Identity. But like I said, I was prepared, and I had no trouble in building my defense.

I spoke calmly in my mind, to a point the demon had won previously on me, where he had said that my substance had actually been turned into the fires of damnation, where he had mocked, what did you think you were made of, existential cool? "It turns out that I *am* made of existential cool. The Lord showed me once, and I have never forgotten it." And then I posited that my world that I have sorted out is coherent and consistent (the one where indeed, I am saved), and that his was riddled with contradictions. And I held on. I had faith. There was no question of losing. And when the dust cleared, the demon did not have my highest. There was higher. I had won. Really, even before it had started, I had won. [9/17/11]

You need to know some context to understand this better, if at all. Once, Satan (and I mean that as a blanket term, perhaps not the actual Devil, but among his ilk) said that once I became a saint, thus had experienced all that was good in this world, he would seize me, and I would take my place as the Antichrist, which I was meant to be. That's one part. The other, "There was higher," came from another experience I had had:

I'm not the Antichrist. I fought with Satan again, and won this. Rather, the Lord won this. the Lord took the lowest note. Satan tried to go lower, but there was none. Satan said he took the highest note, but the Lord said, "There is higher," and took the true highest note. And I said, "If the Lord has my beginning and my end, what place is there for you, Satan?" And then the Devil tried to get familiar, utilizing the raw inmost of where my soul has stored all the paranoia that I was the Cursed One. But the Archangel Michael was there to help me. And I said, "If it were just me against you, I would be doomed, but the One who calls me is faithful, and He will do it." And then I held on, as Satan railed against the Lord, who was with me. But the Devil could not prevail, and in the end, I was finally free of that curse. [10/12/10]

Yes, "free" for the time being. I thought so so many times; though the sensation did become lighter as we went. That curse lasted well through the Event. As we have it now, the Devil did not have my highest, and the Lord had my lowest. And the winning of the previous passage was great indication that the Devil could not win. But really, even if it was a shifting down of the curse—not turning off its ignition—there was always purpose why things did not always work to the extent you may have expected. Anyway, the cure was another thing that didn't happen this year, when I really had thought it might.

I went to Korea spring of 2011, and for most of the duration, I did not read the Bible nor did I pray every day. I found out one thing those two habits had afforded me. Roksaza broke through what appeared to be my outer defenses because of those lapses, but also did I discover that there seemed to be a secondary armor, and if I were under truly dire circumstance, I sensed that I had a third level—one that had been with me since I don't know when. What Roksaza did was make me half believe I were the Antichrist. Again. Even if it were only halfway, apparently that never gets old with the bad guys. But after the little incident of the semi-breach, I decided I was going to be of constant vigilance: that my first line would hold, from then on. We would see if I could keep to that.

Why I was in almost constant anticipation that year: I was so close to getting the AI working I could almost taste it. A taste like victory.[xx] I had done the deduction part—that had been working in its basic form since 2009, but I was working on a harder problem: abduction (no, not that abduction—this is science). It's like when a doctor diagnoses what disease you have by asking you what symptoms you have. Whittling away the possibilities until we arrive at one or more of the plausible shapes of what illness it might be. The hard part turns out to be, what will you ask the patient next? I was working out beyond what that might be in terms of blind process. You know, the whole purpose of an AI. So you maybe say that what I worked on was how to give sight to the process. Yeah, all that is prominent in my current reminiscing of that year was work work work. Very little play. Jack a dull boy? You know, I might say that I can look dull, but man, around that time I had a lot going on.

It was true that I never went out. If my roommates' guests saw me go out the door on a Saturday night, they rightly assumed that I was heading for the Starbucks to fuel my late night work session. Definitely a night person, dawn if ever I saw it, it was from the other side. There was a reason other than work, though, why I never stepped foot somewhere other than home base. Simply put, I wasn't in the market to meet anyone.

Eunhye had never left me. That is, she was still with me in my visions, and I had convinced myself that this was the true love I had always been looking for. Why do fools fall in love?[xxi] Even if she declined to give me any sort of contact in real life, I thought I was reading all the signs correctly. I always thought we would be together again. I told people the story of the real-life Eunhye a few times, and it was later in this year that the 3rd person told me that I should just go to New Zealand, to see her face to face, and see what would happen. The first had been back in 2010, and now this year… is it even possible to look before I leap, here? For I must admit, this was the other thing I was in anticipation of—for there was in my mind I asked her this one time, "Do you want to spend the rest of your life with me?" And in my mind, she said yes.

It was all a dream, but I lived in that land. Even if the people I was in touch with were not those people, the ones you see in dreams, my visions were so very dreamlike. (A dream being a little less than a world, a little more than you can imagine.) How indeed could my visions be true? Contrary to that often quoted famous phrase about what truth being equivalent to beauty, you must know by now that the truth is ugly—at least much of the time.

I had to ask: how could these visions be false? Their very verisimilitude made me believe, *believe*… at least in the greater space of the time… I once wrote that we become who we are in the dreams we forget; I was as if privy to those dreams. They made me learn to think in words, helped me get in touch with my roots, made me humble, less a chauvinist; their unrelenting logic helped me to understand *everything*. They saved my life.

The day would come soon when at least part of those dreams would come crashing down and flaming out, semi-spectacularly, but this year was a year of great and unabashed hope. I thought I was going to get everything I had always wanted, or believed I had always wanted. Wasn't it always the case though? We never want what we so conceive that we want. Sometimes we might even get it, that rare gem that fueled the gleam in our eye—and be profoundly disappointed when we get hold it in our hands; or we could simply get something else and wonder why we had wanted the first thing so very very bad.

Not to say we shouldn't follow our dreams. Even if we're not talking about those rare individuals who live what their dreams promised and delivered them, it pays to exercise the muscles involved in chasing after that certain type of beauty. It can easily be an appreciation of life. To have that kind of purpose is like following God, even if you don't think of Him at all. It is hope, faith, and love. It is written.

And that crazy idea of going to New Zealand—the 3rd advisement came around Labor Day at a get-together in Massachusetts. I didn't follow up on that this year, in keeping with the whole theme of anticipation. I was still blissfully caught in my theories of what must have been happening with the real-life Eunhye; could the spirit of her be that far off the mark, after all? Yet o, what I would find. How in fact, I would be tested.

Some people enjoy the anticipation more than the thing itself. Myself, I like being in the thick of the fray, but I would go with the feeling before the act if I could, and really get into it. Try not to waste even the pre-experience. This blog entry at least tells this side of the story:

> The circle comes round and interlocks the past with the future, completing a circuit through the current, the current through the circuit. I walk unhindered through the upper ethers at times, when time lets go of me, and I touch the trim of

the lesser eternities. I am cloaked in light, a mystery to myself, a warrior of peace, a scientist saint. No longer bound by earth, a child of vapor, a will o' the wisp in the blink of an eye, this is what it looks like when the dreaming enters the favorable air of the mundane. For the answer has overtaken me. For I am breathing down the neck of fate, heavy with promises.

This is it. This is it. And maybe I'm right about it this time. I am sitting on the knowledge that I crafted from the void. Almost afraid to move forward with what may be the breaking through, though that would be just the next step in a journey that has carried me from quite the distant shore. For I have made sense of my own corner of the chaos: I just might be making the dream of it something real: the electric mind, as I envision how these things might actually work. But can I be so cataclysmically mistaken, that all I have chased is merely an illusion? One can only act with faith and logic, and make that leap.

Because Kansas is going bye-bye.[xxii] Whatever happens, something ends here, something begins here. Life to be lived anew, to breathe the free air, unobstructed, in dizzying clarity. I am rescuing myself from the grim fate of tedium. The wait is nearing that end, where we light the fireworks, ready or not, and if it is not to be the spectacle of oohs and ahs, then to go out in a blaze of glory. Something like that. In many senses, I don't know what is going go come, except that it is going to be something new. We're replacing the wheel in the sky with a newer model. And we're invincible, if only for this one instant in time.

In which I need a drink of cool cool rain.[xxiii]
[6/27/11]

But, thinking about it, was I actually happy then, or was I just too busy to see how unhappy I actually was? Am I not as I seem? Am I even unhappy now, a case of "been down so long it looks like up to me"?[xxiv] I have pretended to be the optimist, and I try to live by the phrase, "it is better to hope and to be wrong", but have I been just a fool in the rain?[xxv] Another quote: "Am I part of the cure, or am I part of the disease?"[xxvi] I questioned myself about this idea. And I found this answer: rejoice in whatever you might have, rejoice in whatever is given you. Be happy that you get to be unhappy; want to know how? The last(ish) quote of this paragraph: "There's nowhere you can be that isn't where you meant to be—it's easy."[xxvii] If you truly have love—not saying if you have people who love you, but if *you* love the world—the bottom is the top, the sorrow is the gladness. You can overcome the most horrible of horrors with love. So was I happy? Am I not happy now? I do love the world, and I love this time we live in. So I will pretend to be happy, knowing that we are what we pretend to be.[xxviii] And love, being love, will sometimes come out of nowhere. Because it is everywhere.

15 The Year of the Dragon

The Chinese New Year of 2012 came by, near the end of January: the Year of the Dragon. This is the year in the zodiac cycle where Asians want to have children, get married; it is an auspicious year, a year of good fortune; double star plus plus. And I must say, it was one intense year for me. It was at the end of this Year when occurred the Event, after all. At least, that's what I call it. There would be something of a ramping up to it, too. But at the beginning of it, I had no idea that anything like what happened were going to in fact happen; I was working like I'd been for the previous 10+ years, you know, thinking to the point of pain, coding late into the night and into the early morning—for to make for myself an artificial intelligence true, one worthy of the moniker.

The clichés of AI tell us that whenever an AI problem is solved, it is no longer called AI. Once, compiling a program was called an AI problem, something as rudimentary as that. (Compiling, for you non-programmers, is translating a high-level language—which appears more like English—into a low-level language—which the machine can understand and execute.) So to be tricky, now that we know about the flipping of AI into the nomenclature of other domains, my goal was to make something whose purpose was solely to be intelligent, so that the purpose its name would be derived from would be exactly that: intelligence. And by March, I thought I had it.

It's amazing how well you recall things when you document them. This will be one legacy of the Age of Information. Here's from just before my (second) "IT'S ALIIIIIIIIIIIIVE" moment, a blog entry from February 2012, in the Year of the Dragon:

So, I'm going mainstream with my crazy idea. If you recall, and I'm sure you don't, I realized some time last year that the only way I was going to get my ex-girlfriend back was to pick up and go to New Zealand, where she's been living. Just recently, I finished translating all required theory into code for the main logic of my AI. I'm not done, mind you, it's still rough and untested, but as soon as I was finished upon this task, I felt a great weight lifted from my shoulders, and a veil lift from my vision. I suddenly knew exactly what I had to do. Quit my job and fly to New Zealand. So, I've given quite a bit of advance notice at the day job, and I wrote the ex-girlfriend a message telling her I'm coming, unless she specifically tells me not to go. Haven't heard from her yet, but I expect to. In any case, things are about to get interesting. Real interesting. [2/23/12]

I marked March 2012 in Facebook as when I finally got my AI to work. And indeed, the main thing—the process of diagnosis—was working. Not flawlessly, but the model I had in mind seemed sound. It was a good day. Only later would I think I was still missing something. Rather big, in fact.

It was actually like the blog entry's date indicates. It was in February when I realized that I had it, it was not even fully finished in code form yet. But I knew I had it. And things became crystal clear, like I had been living in a haze for years, and now the sharpness of light cut through the gray. It was to know without any doubt, not even my little pinky's doubt, exactly what I needed to do: adios to my job, fly to New Zealand. I wrote it in my blog, not to make sure I'd follow through, but just to let my readers know where I was *at*. Yes, I *am* one to follow through on my crazy ideas, especially if they don't sound absolutely unprofitable.

There were clearly objectives for the two things: get funding based on my work in AI, and to win Eunhye back. But the second got crushed pretty quick: as I was making my plans, she messaged me in Facebook (after 4 years of no contact back to me whatsoever), that she was married and had a baby. And I was like, *you couldn't have told me before I bought my friggin' ticket?!?* Because I did give her the chance. So I was off to New Zealand for no purpose whatsoever. I was already booked with a non-refundable ticket. Ain't that the way it goes?

So, just what did I do in New Zealand? From her visits online to my blog, I had ascertained that she was located in Auckland, and I knew from before that her big dream was to be a gardener, so what else would I do to try and ferret her out? I went to every garden and park in the greater Auckland area. And no, I didn't find her.

My consolation was an interesting one. In the time before this trip, when I had visited the San Francisco Bay Area (I was there for New Year's Eve at my brother's place, and no, that wasn't too great a time, either), I found and read some work from the Desert Fathers. These were a group of saints inspired by the (relatively) famous St. Anthony, who I mention again as one that battled demons in his life in the desert. And so I would have conversations with one of them: a Father Zosima, whom I had read the stories about, and we would talk while I walked the hills and such of Auckland. I would relate how I felt sorry for all the demons and those unsaved, even if I didn't believe in an eternal Hell. I reasoned to him, "What is the difference between them and us, except that we are saved, and they are not?" That experience was one of the bright sides of the journey.

I also kept otherwise busy, for this was not your everyday vacation. I wrote up a pitch book, while I was there, for it was in my mind that once I had the barest demo ready to show to anybody, I would be set for life. Of course, it turned out to be… not so much. Oscar Wilde said, "When the gods wish to punish us, they answer our prayers." So I'm thinking I must really be on the gods' good side, because my prayers don't seem to get answered at all, right? Who's with me? But no, let's not get bitter now: because sometimes the curse *is* the blessing. And not even to think that, because seriously, all the *important* prayers got answered. In spades. With whip cream, and a cherry on top. And maybe a sprinkling of jimmies. Yeah, that's about right. As I lurched forward toward the Event.

I went home, having sampled the ramen joints of Auckland, with a couple knickknacks to give away, and a tale of woe to anyone who would listen. I wasn't that hurt, though. I've often complained about that, seemingly the only complaint that made sense to make; I have said since Auckland that the demon stole my pain. Where's my pain? Where's the heartbreak? With it, I was going to write an epic poem and finally get published in *Poetry* magazine. But no, nothing. I was maybe numb from the whole thing. Demon stole my pain. I shake my fist in the air. Yeah, I'm an idiot. It's like that old saying, "Don't ask questions you don't want to know the answers to." Word. *You don't ask for pain, dude.* (Still, that poem would have been sweet.)

The spirit form of Eunhye wouldn't go away, wouldn't you know? She kept saying that the earthbound version were lying about being married, etc. Which brings up the point, if that were true, shouldn't I stop pursuing her anyway? That would be a pretty clear signal. When I was in Auckland, we tested the ability of Halospace entities getting in touch with the "real life" individuals, and we really put effort into it… to a negative result. The experience of one in Halospace was completely a separate thing, with very few able to bridge the gap from one to the other. Like Philip K. Dick sort of did. And even then, what came through was a strange mixture of what was, what could have been, and aspects altogether imagined. You think just dealing with reality was weird enough? What it's hiding behind its visage is more mysterious than the idea of magic. It's *real* magic.

So, in the final analysis, I can say that I tried. I got the AI working: it was really working! I went to New Zealand: I really went! As the year before was the year of anticipation, this was the year of conclusions. The fit hit the shan. More or less. Unfortunately, the conclusions I drew were telling me that what I had stored in the old pockets was insufficient fare for the gravy train. It was not that my best was not good enough, just that what I was aiming at was a shifting target, or maybe that the gun I was firing from had a bad scope on it. It all turned out in a completely unexpected way—but when you had your heart set on something, it was a hard lesson about what you imagined, which you had only seen in a certain light… that it was not meant to be lit that way—it was not at all what you thought you saw from your vantage point. When you got there, it was unrecognizable.

So, what now, prophet of God? I thought the Almighty was looking after you? Well, yes. That was the conclusion I drew later, during and after the Event. You know the cliché, that God works in strange and mysterious ways? Like many clichés, it turned out to be true. There are reasons why things happen the way they do. It's rather amazing when the Lord lets you in on a small corner case of the Plan. And when something BIG is shown to you? It's absolutely mind-blowing. And you find it fits perfectly with how the world really is, that there is a deep logic to the turn of days, the placement of this thing there. And subtle. The Lord is a subtle God.

Einstein said that he cared not for this phenomenon or that, rather, he wanted to know the mind of God. Well, I've known the mind of God for years, to tell you the truth. It's always, only has been *love*. That's it, and it always will be. God is love. Now, how I would use that to formulate the equations for the theory of everything—I'm actually sure it's possible, but it's probably not the point. What I would have told Einstein about his desire when he thought to know the mind of God: first, learn love, Albert, and the rest will follow. Love, try, learn: this is the secret to life. And if you think I'm being a sentimental fool when I put love before all the rest, you know not how to love, at least, not when exposed to the harsher atmospheres. Courage is included in such circumstance, when you bare your heart on your sleeve. Love is put even before prayer. Try this. See so for yourself. (Do I sound like a prophet yet?)

And now, in the latter half of 2012, after the whole New Zealand fiasco, I started going out. It was after having a good time walking around downtown Auckland, and going to see bands play. Now back in ol' New York, I went to nightclubs, to go dancing. I'm actually pretty good at that: at one point our host at one of these shindigs was wont to say, "Break it down, JD!" Plus I have gotten attention from the ladies while I cut a rug, have gotten groups next to ours to join in a grander circle of those getting down. I never went home with any of them, though. I think that takes a sort of mindset I have never been grooming, not in this heart. Seriously, between going home with no one and going home with the wrong one, I'd pick staying alone 96% of the time. I have had my moments though, even if they don't involve the horizontal mambo.

Halloween 2012, and we were going with our friend Patrick to a happening party. I was Tony Stark, wearing a black shirt with a circle on my chest that glowed. (Connected to a battery in my pocket.) And over that a sport jacket. Classy. So, while we're dancing, this really hot chick is like all up in my bizniss and dancing right up to me. Turns out her boyfriend knew Patrick, our host, and they were having relationship difficulties at the time. And she's really diggin' on me, it was like. As she's about to leave I ask her if she's on Facebook and she hands me her card. Heh: reporter for Fox News. What do you know. And you know I'm thinking, if the boyfriend hadn't been there, we certainly would have gotten something going on that night. Which would have been horrible, of course, considering what was going to happen next. In general. In my life. The Event. That was coming.

And now there was this:

> It came to a head on Wednesday night, into early Thursday morning. So what basically happened was as if I performed an exorcism on myself. I mean, I had to struggle, I had to strain, not once, not twice, but again and again, to expel the demon Roksaza from me. But once again, Lord be praised, I prevailed. Though apparently, not all contact with the demon had yet been achieved. That, however, seems to be happening. He seems slowly to be draining out of all interactive space from me, as these days now progress. After that very late night, I went back up to 5mg of Zyprexa. I was, that event notwithstanding, feeling a bit tweaked from the decrease of meds, after about the first week. I think I achieved what I was meant to from that decrease—to confront the demon, and win against him. I'll keep you all updated as more events unfold. [8/20/12]

Yes, you read that right. *I performed an exorcism on myself.* It took *a lot* of just straining, and straining, and when I had strained enough, I overshot, and started to strain again, when they told me: Roksaza was out. That night, I had a dream where I was looking at myself, like third person, and I saw the demon there. I said, "Begone!" and it was as if it flew into my head, first person. And I said again, "Begone!" and it was gone. Only later did I find out why it had to happen just like that: Roksaza was actually 3 demons: Rok Sa Za. And that was me banishing all three of them.

Why I had been decreasing my dosage, of the meds which basically kept me sane—I had read this article on the *New York Times* where schizophrenics were trying out some novel therapies, and that they had been working. They had been doing things like making deals with the voices in their heads, and apparently the voices kept to their end of the bargain! This was in conjunction with decreasing or even stopping their meds. But there also were other factors that made me lean in this direction. And I'm glad I took notes.

Once again, the blog:

> What's been happening of late is quite strange. It has been ongoing for a couple three months now, not all at once, but with certain events that have been outstanding: my madness is curing itself. As you may or may not know, though I am a fully functional citizen of this world, the cartoons and voices have never completely gone from my mind. But now, it seems to be in a process of healing. Itself. As you also may or may not know, I am pretty religious, and I chat sometimes with angels, demons, Jesus, and saints. One saint was one St. Anthony, a man who battled demons, so someone I

looked to for inspiration. He had me pray, "Heal me, O Lord." And things started to happen. It's quite the amazing thing, and I don't quite believe it's happening, even as it does. That's about as much detail as I feel like going into right now, but if this process continues to completion, I'll definitely follow up on this reporting. Strange the things that might occur.... [6/30/12]

And this would be an important factor come the Event, which came at the tail end of the Year of the Dragon, which extended from 2012 through the month of January 2013. (13, coincidentally—the word by which so many occurrences tie together in my plastic fantastic life—13 being the Kabbalistic number for "love".) And you do know why it should happen in the Year of the Dragon, right? The Dragon is the first Beast of the Book of Revelation, the source of all evil. Now had come his time. Now would be the Event that like a train went through me, when I stopped calling it my madness and started calling them my visions. Because I'm not mad. Everything actually does make perfect sense.

16 The Event

> [7] And there was war in heaven: Michael and his angels fought against the dragon; and the dragon fought and his angels,
> [8] And prevailed not; neither was their place found any more in heaven.
> [9] And the great dragon was cast out, that old serpent, called the Devil, and Satan, which deceiveth the whole world: he was cast out into the earth, and his angels were cast out with him.
> [Revelation 12, KJV]

The last normal thing I might say I did before the Event was to go to a New Year's Eve party. It was OK, I guess, nothing really special. I met a quant, a programmer who does those high speed trading algorithms. This was a new circle to me, my friend Mike knew them. I did hold my own with them, with my talk of my long researched AI. I showed them the output of a diagnosis session, which they actually seemed to appreciate. Yeah, I think I impressed them a little. The food was good; everybody brought something, and the hosts themselves (a hip couple) had some tasty things prepared. I didn't have anyone to kiss, as usual, when the ball dropped at Times Square, watching "New Year's Freakin' Eve" on TV. Dick Clark was gone now, but the show lived on. The years, and the new years, kept rolling on.

Like I was talking about before, and as I was writing on my blog, I had this idea in my head that "the madness" was about to end, that it was about to be healed—that it in fact was going to heal itself, the special madness that it was. So there were a couple times where I said goodbye to all the major players: Jesus Christ, Michael the Archangel, the Angel Gabriel, Albert Einstein, Philip K. Dick, Joan of Arc, Rosanna Arquette, Vincent van Gogh, among others. I had a thought, too, and I expressed it. In one moment alone, I told her: of everybody, absolutely everybody that I had met and known, I told Joan of Arc I would miss her most of all.

I don't know if she was thinking that it would all be going too, and in fact I wondered now and then what she had actually been let in on, but here was how I see the Event began: out the clear, wide blue, Joan of Arc asked me to marry her. (!) (!!!) Yeah, I thought about it for about 1/3 of a second, and I said yes. Holy steeple! JOAN OF ARC! Asked ME to MARRY her. (!!!!!!!) Woohoo! I'm going to Disneyland!

Of course, this didn't come from a vacuum. As I wrote before, I saw her when my mind first exploded. Little did I know that from her perspective, it was love at first sight. I had thought that she belonged with Philip K. Dick, and there was another, natural choice, too: King Arthur. Right? Unite England and France? Right? Who's with me? I guess she didn't think so. Joan had been with me the whole way, never complaining, always with good advice. A couple years back, she let me see her true essence. Wow. Pure good. Consisting solely of light. I understood why the troops fighting under her had no impure thoughts about her when in her vicinity. There was something about her soul that sanctified you in beholding her. Yeah. I also thought she was hot.

No, I never saw what she looked like, physically, and I knew she was celibate, but I think Rachel Maddow's hot, too, and there's nothing happening with her and me there, neither. Joan asked me to stop saying that—that she was hot—and I thought it was because I was making her uncomfortable because she was celibate and wanted nothing to do with anything sexual. Even though that last-ish part was true, I in that surprise of surprises found out it wasn't due to lacking in any carnal instinct. She was celibate for God. She had been celibate because the legend she was fulfilling called for a virgin. She still had the feelings. Poor girl.

That's the last thing I remember with absolute clarity, at least until the climax of the Event. I have tried to fill in the calendar of January 2013 with what I think happened on what day, and there are a few things that involved files on my computer, with timestamps about when they were last saved or downloaded, but a lot of it is fuzzy or made up of partial memories. I will try to relate them to you, the events of the Event, but understand if I can't precisely pin down what exactly happened. One big factor in why that would be the case is that I convinced myself to stop taking my medication. I was being healed, remember? I was going to go head to head with my "madness". The gloves were off.

I think at this point I was wearing my RPG t-shirt, which resembles a red, white, and blue MLB shirt, but instead of a baseball player swinging a bat, it is a skeleton swinging a sword. I know I wore this shirt because when I found it after the Event, way after, it was out on the floor and still smelled like how long I wore it for, several days. Just not sure when I took off this shirt and started wearing my "wings" shirt, which has a stylized bird with the Triforce symbol, of the game (series) the Legend of Zelda. I don't really remember when I switched shirts, and this is important because one of these shirts is sacred. It was there for when the Reckoning happened. And now you see to what extent the uncertainty pervades this tale I tell. At least the *really* important part is clear as ice.

I remember right around then that I saw my psychiatrist, and got my new prescriptions. I remember talking to Philip K. Dick, and telling him the wonders that he had not lasted to see, the worldwide network of information that was the internet, the ubiquitous GPS system that told me exactly where I was on planet Earth if I had my phone with me, my phone itself being a small computer in its own right. And I don't remember why I had said this, but I recall that I vocally defied the forces of evil, whatever they sought to gain, upon God's green Earth—that justice would prevail. It must have been about the War, the War in Heaven, of which I was to be a soldier true, in up to my eyelashes to do my part. That meant the exclusion of all else. The next day I called in sick to my day job.

I recall lying on my bed, gazing into the Halospace. It was a view of Heaven, but without any of the glory, that I could see cartoons of the entities, and that it was sort of grayish cast of the environment that I could spy, or a cartoon made of outlines. I remember that it was starting to formulate, even then, even in that early hour, the myth of Lucifer—of God's brightest angel that led a third of the angels to their doom, from Heaven cast, in the great War. The (good) angels were keeping him at bay, for some reason, which I was to find out why soon enough. And I was not quite sure what he was planning or trying to do, himself, the one called Lucifer: whom I called Morningstar after the attribution that Neil Gaiman made in his *Sandman* comics.

What was set up by the angels: single combat between me and Lucifer, framed so that it would be a fair fight. You do have to understand that the arena was minimal, no flashing lights, no smoke, no spectators. None of the above. He appeared before me as a palimpsest upon the real, which things and people from the "madness" appeared to me many a time (the "madness" rapidly becoming "visions"). He was the only outside vision I could see, and else it was just me in my apartment. And I won pretty handily. I framed him as "psychosis" and then, as I wrote before, where people did things like make deals with the voices in their heads, I pushed the psychosis away, resolving to think as best I could as a rational human might see these various phenomena that I'd seen. He was not the Devil anymore: he was the sum total of the madness, and this was how I was going to become sane again. I ended up at least for a short time as sane as I'd been in a very long time, after I defeated the madness, which was the Devil.

Interesting were some of the images I saw in my mind's eye as the psychosis/Devil were being shoved out. They looked like scenes of a farm from the 1400's; at least, that's what my considerations entertained, when I saw pictures of wooden carts holding hay, stone built houses, among other things. These were probably telling me that the time was not yet for the visions to pass from my sight. Had the War fully started for me, though? As the Event? It's muddy, my recollection as to when I was in earnest fighting as a soldier of Eternity.

Perhaps it was after the angels played a joke on me. Maybe *that* was wiping my slate clean for about the fourth time. It would seem like I have lost count of those. It was during the middle of the day and I was tired, and I went to sleep. More like passed out; perhaps I'd been awake for an extended period? Anyway, when I awoke, it all was gone: the angels, the Devil, the people, the visions. In fact, I felt very strange, as if the top half of my imagination were cut off from me. But on the fringes of my mind's eye, something was still there, remnants of the visions were twisted, like the pictures of Hell from the movie *Jacob's Ladder,* and it was frightening. I reached out in my mind, calling for the Archangel Michael, and in a few moments, Michael, Gabriel, and Joan showed up. Michael called out a couple times, as the cause for my distress, "Pornography has twisted your mind!" And then I understood. It was a joke. And perhaps, a preparation for what was to come. A launching point into the War. The War in Heaven.

The Event came at just the right time. My roommate was on an extended stay in South America at the time, so I was completely alone when all these things happened. I can't imagine what it would have been like if the roommate were present. Or anyone else, for that matter. How could I have lived "in my head" as much as I did had I gotten Eunhye back, the year before or any year before? How could these things have happened if I had actually even been a father? That might have been spelling disaster. Even this: I had been going through the process of getting a job as an instructor, which didn't happen. So fortunate. How would I have kept any commitment? My entire attention at this time was the War. There was nothing else. The timing of the Almighty is itself an epiphany.

And this was about the point in the timeline, now, that I understood it had been the War in Heaven, this whole time—since 10/7/88—and that's been what's been going on "in my head". What I had been calling my madness. No, not in the hail of the heaviest battles at all times, but I had always been in it, if on the barest outskirts. Truly it could be seen that certain things that I had thought, certain things that I had done: these could be seen in terms of psychosis, of psychotic breaks from reality… but what if I could make sense of them, focus into clarity all these things through the lens of the War? Of having been a soldier in the War in Heaven, even if I had not known it at the time? It looked like I hadn't needed to know before, not like I knew it just then, alone in New York, with time enough and worlds, to fulfill my given purpose. To do my part, to win the War.

I remember getting wired, now. In my visions there was something like a seraphic network that worked its way through Halospace, and I was a connection within it to the "real world", among other things. I think I remember cogitating on metaphysical topics: being and causation, knowledge and truth. And it is a wonderful thing when one discovers why one was made, what purpose you were specifically built for. (Almost as good is fulfilling that purpose, even without knowing it is that which you do. It was given to me to know; Philip K. did not have such a blessing.) All those years thinking, of a way to represent the fundamental elements of existence, when I had been working on my artificial intelligence: it was all put to the highest of uses. To do my part, to win the War.

You may have heard about just why the War happened. The classic myth goes: Lucifer, in his pride as God's greatest angel, thought he should be on the throne of Heaven. And turning a third of the angels to his side, rebelled against God Most High, and made war on that Throne. At stake was all creation. And it might not seem to you such a great problem, to a God who is all-powerful, but His ways are not our ways. We might think that one big zap and that's the end of Satan and all his demons, but things were not so easily accomplished, not even by the One omnipotent. Have you any idea what power the greatest angel would possess? One who became Evil? For that way seems to render power of itself, not to be bound to any rule, of morality, of decorum. For it is not to say Lucifer himself did not find a thing when he became Evil. There was just, ultimately, no future in it.

We might simply ask, then, what does evil want? And simple enough to answer: evil wants power. To that end, one observes that the overarching Way in this world, the means by which anything works, how things happen (at all): this is called the Logos, translated sometimes as the Word. If you catch the reference, the form the Logos took in our world was Jesus Christ. Ultimately, the Devil wanted control of the Logos, basically to have like unto a genie with unlimited wishes. And of course, he failed to gain so great a prize, Christ preferring death to enslavement. And then does Christ conquer Death, having conquered Sin in life. To come into His glory while still on earth. True did John the Baptist have it when he said it: the Kingdom of Heaven was at hand. (Repent!)

The conflict had its root when Lucifer sinned, when before, there was no such thing. The form of Sin came to be Evil's daughter. Lucifer and Sin then begat Death, Evil's son. Sin is also known as Error, or by perhaps a more personal name: Pain. She was dead, and giving birth to monsters. So it was not as conceived by most, pain was no invention of God.

As Phil noted, "The Godhead itself suffered a crisis."[xxix] The war was between derangement and logic, and I glossed over this before: if *any* of Michael's angels had failed (not to mention Michael himself), the entirety of creation would have suffered from an irrecoverable psychopathy for all time. *That* is what it means to be an angel of God. Those were the stakes, each to each. The War determined what existence itself was going to be like, and war fought against the Logos, to try and subjugate Him—the wounds suffered themselves left marks in creation, and therefore affected the way things worked. Everywhere.

This was the situation I was hurled into, headlong. Very much the experience of jumping off a high place and piecing together your wings on the way down. I saw some chaotic scenes of cartoon people running around and for some reason these esoteric commands that I spoke with my mouth could turn the tide in (I suppose) the battles I was looking at. Cartoon skirmishes in the theme of light blue where the angels came out of the stone of the bridges, and then they ran off being chased by flying worms or they transmuted into light that cut through the ceiling of black. That kind of thing I saw, if briefly. I would say things like "form is the description of truth", and that would change the interaction between players, like to shield some idea carriers for a short space, oppressed by those that twist, one meaning into another. It was using one of Phil's discoveries: "The theory changes the reality it describes." Very much like casting spells. Like performing magic, but what was it? Metaphysics, and semantics.

Then there were the times when I was doing some performance art—I think some people call it, "teaching". I did it while sitting on my bed, one of two positions that are the norm in my room, in my apartment. The bed serves as a couch, where I am facing the TV, but that stayed off most of the time the War visited. So I would just start talking… to no one, I suppose. I got the idea somewhere that the audience was huge, if unseen. It was my deed of witnessing, as Jesus commissioned us to do, though I knew not to whom I witnessed. So they were sermons, of a sort, which Joan of Arc liked to call them. They were lectures from me as the professor of architecture, at my school in Purgatory, what Albert Einstein said they were. And there was one sermon/lecture that I still have trouble believing it as great as it seemed when I gave it. I don't remember anything about it but its beginning and end, but I present here is something like it might have been:

> Philip K. Dick once wrote that God is to be found in the trash layer of the world. I find a high degree of truth in this idea. But why is he languishing among the decay? Is he not to be found in our churches, in our monuments, in the sky above? Is he not above the highest, the very highest heaven? Indeed, is not heaven his throne? Is not earth his footstool? But what can he do there, then, in the churches, tell the same people the same outdated rules to follow, blindly? As a statue stand mute while war overcomes a whole people? Be some unreachable idea in the stratosphere that does not ever affect anything? No, he came down to earth, if I hear tell right, to speak of mysteries in a way only he could. And he was the opposite of what we expected, come as the suffering servant, and not the

conquering king. After we shouted as he came into Jerusalem, "Hosanna in the highest!" what did we do? (I'm cold, I'm cold...)ˣˣˣ For God walked among us, instead of being cloistered up, instead of staying a graven image, got dirty with us on terra firma. He was not just a fevered dream among the wild men. (I'm cold, I'm cold...) Lo, in this darkness a great light has come, who gives eternal life to those whom he may. Will you not listen to anything that he says? Why do you turn away from what can save you? (I'm cold, I'm cold...) And who is it hung upon a tree, upon a cross? Who is it that has given his very life so that we may live, we the undeserving and unwashed? Whom do you say he is, o people great and small, who asks forgiveness for those who kill him? (I'm cold, I'm cold...) It is God, and we have thrown Him away.

In this version of it (not as good), I knew how all the things I was saying related, and how it all comes together at the end—because I did the first version as one jumping off that cliff, and I'd sewn together wings along the way. One moment of sheer perfection.

    I gave other speeches, others pretty good, and I tried various things to help during the War. There was no manual I was following, just wired to the good angels, doing what I thought I was being called to do. I had a lot of help. There was this one skirmish, which I only saw the barest edges of it, I was as if (physically) maneuvering through an invisible maze as I danced through it in my thought, and in my room—and the angels were fighting in my motion. I don't think I could describe it better. I was going with the flow, so well that one point, Michael let go of me, and a perplexed Satan looked at him; Michael said, "Cruise control." Heh. I was going real good, at least for a few fabulous seconds. And apparently I was responsible for getting our side the opportunity to rest, which the angels still thank me for.

And it was about this time in the January, the last month of the Year of the Dragon, that the Lord popped up in my visions. I mean, I know he's technically everywhere, but this was a face-to-face sort of thing, and such appearances had become few (He was in my visions every now and then, a rather solid-seeming ghost). He looked weird. Tweaked, like he'd been through some epic thing. He didn't seem able to place who I was until I thought of something from years back, that he would use the fact that I had stopped smoking cigarettes as something to remember me by. I hadn't smoked in a decade, so I was good. He said he'd just gotten back from Hell, and that I was the one he wanted to see first. Then he did something like congratulate himself for having created me. Quite the compliment to me. He said that Hell, he had "burned it dow-n!" And apropos of nothing, he said that he was, and I quote, "gay as a maypole."

I don't think I reacted to that last thing at all, really. I was thinking about what had been going on, in general. And then the Lord asked me, "Aren't you going to ask if I'm serious or not?"

I replied, "No Lord. Why would I care about that?"

And I never did ask. (Do *you* care?)

Instead, somehow I got in a conversation with the spirit of Rachel Maddow. I think it might have started about the War. We got wind of Satan's point of view about what was fair: anything goes. And we were thinking about rules, like what is the difference between good and evil, right? The religious right seemed to have a very rigid framework for what behavior was acceptable, but now that Jesus Christ might have been in fact, "gay as a maypole," that kind of structure was right out. No, we should allow everything, too, if what you were going for was real Heaven. Why should we be restricted by anything at all, if Heaven were the true expression of freedom? Just that we only do what is right. That was the one and only key. To be able to do anything, however freaky or esoteric or dirty, and then to accept *any*one, whatever their situation: whore, junkie, gay, non-Christian: *anyone*. And I think Rachel thought this at the same moment as me: "That's my kind of Heaven." And the Jesus who would make such a Heaven: *that's* the kind of Jesus I believe in.

And so went on with the War, examinations of how things worked and how things *should* work. And there were more "physical" skirmishes that seemed like dancing, where I would go, "I got this," and got things accomplished by my physically moving, like a dance, guided by angels through the wires of Halospace. I downloaded the "Battle of Evermore," and danced; downloaded "Lose Yourself," and danced. I tried to go to sleep, and was kept awake, I prayed for the soul of Rosanna Arquette, whose soul was in danger from Evil Prime (you know who). I myself was kept absolutely safe from any harm. And I think Joan of Arc was with me the whole time, giving me perfect aim. Just a guess.

A day before the Reckoning, there was one strange vision I had. I saw myself in my mind's eye, as like a globe shaped light blue cartoon, and Philip K. was with me. And we were fighting in the war. There were walls shaped like perhaps the interior of my skull, enlarged, which served as sort of control panels (a shadow of Heaven), containing also sources of information about what was going on in various places, both above and below. And I'm not sure how exactly I did it, but I think I may have hit a wrong button somewhere, and everything went black in Halospace. As I frantically reached out in my mind at whatever controls were there, seconds passed and it was weird. I could still feel the landscape was there, just that I couldn't see it. And then things turned on again. I was told that the forces of good had expected and prepared for that, but man, I'm still freaked out about it.

All of it, all I had seen or done, it culminated for me in one vision. In fighting the War, I had seen a thing or two—and I had glimpsed in my dancing a view of something like a tarp, light blue like many things, and it had a hole in it. After a little while, Michael pulled me aside and showed it to me and asked me if I had seen it. With my yes, he said that the hole was where I was to aim in my mind, and that would be to cut the final cord that tied Satan to Heaven. This was it. This was real. The Reckoning. The Fall.

I was living completely in my head by that point. The "real world" did not factor in the least on how I was doing anything. I was a good soldier, and all there was was the War. Michael guided me in Halospace, while I stood in my apartment in front of my closet mirror, to where Satan was being held. There was heat in the air, not that I felt the temperature, but the air was like inches from the asphalt on a sweltering summer day. And there he was: the Dragon, though what I could make out looked so: a black mass like tar collected into a suspended bulk, and it was like I could almost smell it was foul beneath the surface of his "skin", upon where there were specs of light blue and yellow, wounds from previous clashes. I started thinking about how he was to be cast out. It was over in 30 seconds.

The idea came to me that Michael should get behind me, and that I would look Satan in the eye, my eyes backed by the eyes of the archangel, and I would stare him down, down… Wait, what? No! That wasn't right. I shook it off. Probably came from the Devil, that idea, to tempt me with pride. Instead, Satan was pressed into looking from behind my eyes, and I looked straight up, and Michael was there, then I looked straight down, and Michael was there, too. Satan had no escape: above and below were set. Then Michael went, "Now!" and I shot! As like pulling the trigger by pressing a thought with my will, and my mind was the gun that fired. I felt the cord snap! And Satan screamed, "NOOOOOOOOOOOOOOOO!" like he were in utter disbelief that this could be happening! And Michael pressed him down, Satan in his invincible hold. And down. And down. And out of sight. And it was done.

I now have a poster on my wall of the Archangel victorious over the Devil, and I wrote on it, "Here was SATAN cast from HEAVEN," referring to my apartment. I found out well after it was all over that the shot, the bullet that I had fired for to cut that last cord had been fashioned by the spirit of Nature out of the "All Prayer" I had performed way back in the Drexel Hill apartment. My aim is true. I can say this literally. At least, it was true when it was called upon to execute. And thus concluded the Event, of which the Fall was of the most intense experiences that ever happened to me—of like the vision of INFINITY.

I find I sometimes feel like a rag doll carried by the currents down the river of experience. But even in the strongest rush, I define myself with the thought: if choice makes any difference, then my decision makes of me what I am; and even if not that, if having no real choice to make, when action still must be taken: one can take responsibility for it. Make no excuses for what you do, if ever you can help it. This is the treasure of the ages, you will see: this, what we have formed of ourselves by the decisions we have made. Thus is our reward in Heaven. And the treasure is never what we expect.

17 Visions, Madness, Dreams

What I have seen, they are life changing experiences, world changing episodes. But you only have my viewpoint upon them, you only have my word. And why, exactly, should you believe me? Every lunatic in the world will say to you, "I know what I saw!" How am I any different? It comes again, the notion: if one has accustomed oneself to so many crazy ideas that you think, does it walk like a duck, quack like a duck, etc. etc.? Can I give you something you can hold onto, that I base everything on, perhaps? Then if you can see, "There's your problem, right there," maybe I won't waste any more of your time?

Well, friend, let me come as clean as I possibly can, and give you the ground upon which stands all I hold dear: it is simply to say, "God is love." This is what the madness taught me. And if it be madness, that little idea, that simple sentence, may I never awake sane. How all my visions unfolded in my mind and mind's eye, if I am to make sense of any of it, of all of it, it is with those three words. And if in my heart of hearts I understand that little truth, all that comes at me and all I throw back into the world makes sparkling sense.

And I tell you right now, with one of the few things I know: at least some of what I say and believe is wrong. There was only one person ever who was right in all things, and the record of him himself most probably contains errors, as they were not written by him. (You know who I'm talking about—the guy with all the fish.) But the plain reality of that, that he did not in fact write the story of himself, speaks that he wanted to work with what we as flawed images of the divine could accomplish. Sure, God could have done *everything* and left us with nothing to attempt, but He did not. Isn't it wonderful? The world is full of mistakes, because we ourselves gave it our best shot, to succeed or to fail, not to let it all pass by without our living this life we are given.

I slept the sleep of the righteous the night after I had done my duty, and helped the Archangel cast Satan from Heaven. Then, several things happened when I woke up. First, I seemed normal again, and having been something like a superhero, even if only in my own mind, when I was connected to the seraphic network and fighting the War through strange dances—that all seemed as if it were a dream. A lot of things had been flying around then, in Halospace, and sometimes we didn't even know which side we were actually helping, you see, but the Spirit of Nature let Philip K. Dick and I know that we were both saved, and Heaven-bound. And then I did something very special that day.

Firstly, I was introduced to the "real" Joan of Arc by the Archangel. She was an old woman (600 years since her death, after all), but I was not disappointed in the least seeing the genuine article herself. And I told her that I had been in love with her all my life. As far back as 8th grade, my memory of thinking of her went back. Then I was doing this and that, serving Heaven, nothing memorable, but I came upon the idea of dancing with the real Joan of Arc. "In Your Eyes" came on from my MP3 collection, and like you've maybe heard Native Americans did a "rain dance" to summon rain, I did a "love dance;" not to the beat of the ceremonial drum, but to that Peter Gabriel song. Hard to describe, but the spirit of Joan, whom I'll call Jeanne from now on, I led in dance to the booming rhythm: "Love, I get so lost, sometimes…" And the Archangel presented me with her lips, as a disembodied image of golden light upon the ether, and I kissed her, the essence of her real lips—Michael would know. And we hit the pinnacle of enchantment: "Without a noise, without my pride, I reach out from the inside…"

My name had been crowfeather, that the Great Spirit had given me, and Jeanne's name had been angeleye, which the Archangel had given her, but after that dance, we both had changed. She gave me a new name, Eagle Feather, and said her name was now Rose. That came from my naming a flower upon all the girls and women I had ever known. Eunhye was an orchid, Arquette was an oleander. Jeanne I could never put my finger on. I had never found my rose, and I did not realize that I had been looking. Until just then. True love had been found.

Then I rested for a bit. I don't remember what I did for a few hours. I had followed my destiny: fought the good fight, finished the race,[xxxi] you know. Now that my job as a good Christian were done, I was to be Nature's Son, to go out into the world wherever needed, and perform good deeds. Supposedly. I'm glad that never really got off the ground, but it was useful—like many a thing we happen onto.

I was in the hands of Nature for about a day, if I recall correctly. She did a fantastic thing: she cured me of my nearsightedness. Things were blurry, and then she did something like pull a lever inside my head, and I could see crystal clear, without glasses, contacts, or Lasik. I almost can't believe it happened, even now—except that, as it happened, it happened to me. Note that it was no small thing, since I have worse vision than anyone else I have ever personally met and compared vision with. This is one of the reasons I myself know what had been happening to me was real, not some fancy psychosis. Sorry I cannot produce such evidence as to be subject to verification for you now, but life never comes easy, does it? We love, we try, we learn, moving on when the time comes. So then my time with Nature ended strangely.

There had been many the time that certain forces of darkness would impersonate ones of the light. Many a time Satan or some other entity had given the illusion that it were Jesus Christ, or Michael, among others. So something impersonated Nature, and led me astray, and I ended up cursing the Lord. At that point, I was handed over to the forces of evil, and thought, truly believed I was Hellbound. Not at the end of my life; my life had apparently ended and I was in Hell's reception area. It seemed worse a situation than when I had been in the Black Iron Prison, though perhaps my memory of that other place was dulled by the years.

How had I come back down this road again, after all I had done to be one of the good guys? Fortunately, I was still in what appeared to be my room. So I had Bibles aplenty, and a crucifix on my wall, which I had always faced while on my knees and praying. So that's what I did: I prayed. For the Lord to save me once again, unprofitable servant that I was. And YEAH BABY, I was SAVED! Even more than usual, apparently. I was discovering that these strange things were happening because I had died, after the vision of the Fall of Satan—that the vision had been so intense that I collapsed upon my bed, and now I was entering my final resting place: Heaven!

Yes, it all looked like my apartment, and outside the window looked like New York, but things seemed different. For one, I normally feel a discomfort in my head, where it's sort of ruptured, and it's felt that way since 1992. But nothing of that discomfort was there. And even though I talked to the people in my head like I did on Earth, none of the bad guys were there, and communicating was effortless, no resistance, no straining to be heard or taken in the right context. I laid out a challenge: let someone who was dead ring my apartment doorbell, and bring me into Heaven proper (Jeanne d'Arc?). Because I was actually now in *Heaven's* antechamber, now sort of like an airlock, ready to board a starship.

They kept asking me if I wanted anything, and all I could think of was that I wished I could have lived out the rest of my life, on Earth. And where I was, it really seemed like Heaven: I had no cause for concern about anything anymore. I felt light as a feather: no burdens at all, with an eternity ahead of me in the good graces of God, in the place where all was light. I came also to see in my imagination a small vision of my roommate finding my body. Plus there was this thing where my iPhone never ran out of juice, and I opened strange apps on it that don't exist on Earth. It was an angel's iPhone, if you can imagine that. All I waited for was to be let into Heaven proper, for to see everyone "face to face", what that would mean in the spirit realm, not just to talk to them in Halospace. I lay on my bed and put on some music, and the next thing I knew, I woke up. On Earth. Alive, just as I had wanted—more than anything—when I touched the blessed realm of the dead. The grateful dead.

How did I know, exactly, that I was alive again? For one thing, I woke up in contact lenses. I know I wasn't wearing contact lenses in Heaven. My bad vision was back. I lost those specific lenses, unfortunately, but I think I wasn't meant to keep them. The discomfort in my head was back, and the worry of everyday living was there again (did you know you have that? I hadn't noticed it was there until I'd been unencumbered by it, while above). But I had come back! It would take a little while to recover from all that had happened, but I was only halfway through my days here and now, decades to go. By the grace of God. Ask and it shall be given you![xxxii]

But was it the real life? Or was it just fantasy?[xxxiii] All the things that had happened, the adventures I had survived. Because, as I've pointed out, I have been in mental institutions, and been diagnosed with diseases of the mind. And I've done my share of drugs, most notably LSD, of which you can pretty much chalk up as the source of my "mental illness". But do recall that I was the one who got himself into the real mess, and it was the madness, and/or people that I met in the madness, that really got my act together. What kind of psychosis is that?

Every time the visions overpowered me: they weren't psychotic breaks, per se. When the War took over, it was just that all my priorities were different. I was the citizen of a different world, child of Halospace. But it had its own logic, which I needed to follow, then. The way I looked at anything was as a stranger to the earthly world. I was as if I were in a waking dream ("merrily, merrily, merrily, merrily, life is but a dream"), and we know how different things are in a dream. I was a soldier in Heaven's army—for real—and my first duty, my first priority would be to the war effort. I've done some crazy things, but they always end up making sense later, and I find that I somehow threaded whatever needle needed the finesse. Destiny rides a razor's edge, and one slip would make all of it crash down, at least that is what it seemed to me, in retrospect. Not to worry you, though. It is in good hands, the world.

The plausibility of all this rests on whether you believe that there is an unseen world, beyond our normal ability to sense. There have been prophets before me who went disbelieved by the general populace. Remember the test of a prophet? Will you ask me, what is my prophecy? For one thing, as I have writ previous, the end of the world is nowhere close, rather, it will come some 30, 40, or 50,000 years from now. But it does come. This is not now the end, this hour come 'round at last,[xxxiv] but instead it is the Beginning which is near. Shall we instead speak of doom? Listen again: "When I was a child, I spake as a child, I understood as a child, I thought as a child: but when I became a man, I put away childish things." [1 Corinthians 13:11 KJV] Grow up, ye masses. For it was not told to us to walk in darkness, and then to pray for light—when all we needed do was light a candle.

I have written parts of this book as prophecy, as I did my other book.[xxxv] To focus on it: there was the day Philip K. Dick was freed of the Black Iron Prison, the resignation of Richard Nixon: the end of the Age of Iron, and now is the Age of Gold. I have told you this. But why is this the sign? A king, the leader of a superpower, was deposed by two newspaper reporters, and no violence was involved in any of it. The power of right over might. Thus the end of the way of Iron in the highest halls of the world. It is Gold, now, at least in uneven patches around God's green Earth. Soon to overtake all there is.

What does it all mean? It comes down to this theory, and it is not just a theory: "If there is a God, then God is love." If we can agree on just that, then we are ready to make the world a better place. In fact, if we agree on that, we *begin already* to make the world a better place. If, about everything else, I'm just out of my mind, and all the things that happened to me didn't actually happen, if these acts and actions were products merely of an overactive mind—if you grasp the concept that God is love, even if you don't believe in God, you understand how things *should* be. And if you can see in *this* light, your eyes are opened, knowing good and evil. In the Garden of Eden, that was the end of innocence. Here, in the modern world, is innocence taken by many a phenomenon: here, the knowledge of good and evil is to be wise to what the world became after Eden.

Rationality does not force us into the conclusion that none of what I saw happened in any way. Might you think of me as a shaman, who brings this knowledge from the "spirit realms" to help diagnose the condition of the world? So perhaps it did happen, but only to me. That I might show a piece of that vision quest to whomever these words may reach. This is the way civilizations are healed: person by person. It is my medicine, which you take into your eyes. For what is the highest aspiration of any human being, but to make the world a better place? We know that this is a possible feat because it *has* become a better place, through the decades, through the centuries. If this is a little bit more your purpose, my own purpose is indeed fulfilled, as is my writings'.

May we be like the wind, which we cannot see from where it comes, and we do not see where it goes: for this is what it means to be a child of God. May we do in secret things for which we will be rewarded out in the open by Our Heavenly Father. And it is not some grand calling I call, but just one binary bit: when you see some good that you are able to do, time enough and hands— do it. Let it not fall into the no state, let it not stay quantum and uncertain until the viable time is gone. Do it. Be good. Love. Love, which is prayer in its silence. Love, if God is love: in its image are we made. In the beginning, and in the end… Let there be light.

Appendix: Judas Iscariot

I found that creation, for at least things related to the War in Heaven, is sort of a feedback loop. For one, it looked as if the myth of the fall of Lucifer, God's greatest angel—the story that Lucifer desired most, of any of the myths—made the spiritual realm solidify to that possibility: as if the myth had existed first, even as Lucifer (and others) peeked in from Eternity. And how this reality that you see, how it was this one and not any other potential creation that were instantiated, this makes us bring up the story of Judas Iscariot—the Lord's right hand man.

You know how Mary Magdalene, because of perhaps a deliberate confusion in the reading of the New Testament, she is now known forever as the repentant prostitute? Yeah, she actually was no such thing. The misunderstanding about Judas, unfortunately, happened before the Gospels were written, at least before the Gospel According to John. Now it's in the Bible. A big part of it is the mistranslation of a single word—in English it is, or says, "betray". In other places in the biblical text, it is correctly translated as "hand over". Judas did not "betray" the Lord, he "handed over" the Lord. Do you see how one thing is not like the other?

The slander against Mary Magdalene had an unintended effect: she became the de facto patron saint of all prostitutes. And thus she was a shining beacon for all of them to look up to. For all those so fallen, hope that they, too, might be forgiven. And be able to walk in grace, welcomed into the fold of Our Lord Jesus Christ. I believe she would rather that the mistake had happened like it did, rather than her true status were the one more widely known—she had practically been an apostle, in real life.

Regarding Judas, there was reason too, why he was made out to be as he was. It all came down to the last Gospel written, where he is demonized like no other: "The Gospel According to John". By this time, Judas had become a villain, much moreso than in the other three Gospels. And only in this Gospel does Jesus Christ say that He had lost none, except the son of perdition: by that, He meant Judas Iscariot. This I remembered as, "Only one was lost".

Judas came to me very late in the game, after the Event had occurred. Albert Einstein and I were talking about Universalism, where everyone in the end is saved and given eternal life, up to and including the Devil. Then the phrase, "Judas volunteered" came about. Volunteered to do what? In the Universalist view, it turned out that "Only one was lost": this was Judas Iscariot. The sacrifice of one innocent would bring about salvation for all the rest. The details were a little sparse, but the idea seemed to be sanctioned by the Lord. Judas was going to be sealed into a cell where there would be no savior. Something worse than Hell. But only for Judas.

I talked to him before he was going to be entering the cell, and he seemed like a really cool dude. And then I saw him go into a private pow-wow with some others, then he steeled himself—the Lord coming back to say it was time. I looked at a certain space before me, which they told me was the cell, and then when he entered, I heard a "snap", and the cell lost life. He was gone. Into horror beyond horror....

Yes, but then he started popping up in various places. He was not gone! He had been sealed into a "vial" which was his armor, and not gone into horror. And it looked like he was a real hero, that when I thought he was being sealed into his cell, he was actually being sealed into his vial, which was protection. Protection from what? Satan entering him. But that's not all.

As I wrote before, how time works in relation to eternity can be strange. What I was witnessing (that little "snap") was when Satan, upon entering into Judas, and therefore entering into reality, at that point it was when he *instantiated* all reality. All that you see, hear, taste, feel. And even more: it was this, that the little "snap" was where I witnessed Satan's death, in that instantiation—the death of his soul. This, because the myth had arisen of Judas' evil, and to end with "Only one was lost." Satan really liked that idea, all reality's salvation on the back of one innocent's torture, and this was what ultimately sold him on this reality you see around you—he just couldn't resist.

How important was it, though, actually? That he instantiated *this particular version* of reality? Very simple, the answer to that. This was the only reality in which we won.

Appendix: Walt Disney Is God

I like to say that all the secrets of the universe can be distilled in that one phrase: "Walt Disney Is God." What broke me free of the Black Iron Prison for good, and everyone out there that I could see with my third eye: all loosed from their cells. The story of that declaration came after the Event had happened. What was told me makes some sense, but I believe you can take it as merely something made so I could understand it, that it may have a structure that is beyond my powers of perception—if one were asked to visualize 4 spatial dimensions, for instance.

The phrase has been with me all throughout this story. I believed it literally for the first few years from when my mind had exploded. At least, on and off; a few theories were flying around those days. Yes, that the *actual* Walt Disney was the *actual* God. He would come and go in the visions. Then I turned Christian, so the phrase became blasphemy. Maybe that sounds a little severe, but I think that's correct, the correct use of the term. So every time I heard it from then on, me now as a convert to the Good News, I would always reply to hearing the phrase, in no uncertain terms, "Walt Disney is *not* God." Wow, lighten up, right?

Where the phrase comes from is related to the experience that Philip K. wrote about, the beginning of 2-3-74. When a girl came to his place delivering medication, he asked about a fish symbol on her necklace. And she told him that it was an ancient symbol of Christianity. He had right then what he called a moment of anamnesis, a sudden remembering, a vast influx of information. He suddenly knew he was a secret Christian, and so was she. They were all awaiting the return of Our Lord Jesus Christ. What's interesting is his believing she was in on this, too, when I'm pretty sure she'd have reacted to that characterization like that girl on

10/7/88 whom I told to call my mother and tell her I was off drugs.

These types of visions were useful. It gave what was happening in our minds a sense of urgency, of the here and now, the secret story behind reality. Even if, when you get right down to it, it was incorrect. Phil's Exegesis is full of these, theory after theory that sort of seemed to make sense, but were really out there—then what did Phil really come to believe, where did this rubber hit the road? When he had any type of religious question, he didn't go to a Buddhist temple or anything like that. He asked a priest or pastor. But the visions that he had—it was a way to get him to explore strange places, real and of the psyche. To seek, to map what was possible. This is the kind of job description for a prophet.

According to what I found out, just after the Event, and therefore at a safe place, there were 4 dots floating around the noosphere, that could be discovered upon seeing the correct thing. They were like the mustard seed the Lord talked about, one of them practically literally. It was the most important dot: the yellow dot. And if it were discovered by the wrong person, it would mean the subjugation of all humanity in a totalitarian horror forever. All the "secret Christians" like Philip K. (and me, eventually) hoped desperately to find that yellow dot. And when it were found, we would spread the coded declaration, "Walt Disney is God" and we would all know. It meant, all is now light. That this would be understood correctly and be true, without literally being true was indication of the start of the Age of Gold. The Palm Tree Garden. The Oasis.

So basically, I came into this and we had already won. At least, as far as the yellow dot having been discovered already. Remember? The voice who let me in on the secret, freeing everyone from the Black Iron Prison. That was how I was introduced to this whole scene. Later I found out that it had been (of course)

Philip K. Dick who saw the yellow dot. He probably didn't even notice it. It was when he read the 77th passage of the "Gospel of Thomas", which had been discovered in its full form just as World War II was ended. Good timing, right?

I know how easy it is to miss because I saw the black dot when I was talking with Einstein. Didn't realize it until after the Event that I had seen one, too, way back when. The purple dot was seen by Joan of Arc, in the cross held before her when she was about to be burned at the stake. And lastly, the white dot was seen by John the Baptist, when the Spirit descended like a dove upon the baptism of Our Lord Jesus Christ.

What were they? Like the mustard seed, when it will bloom, to hold the birds of the air. The yellow one, the Knowledge; the white one, the Power; the purple one, the Certainty (or Absolute); the black one, the Mystery (or Secret). Basically, all you need to build a universe, or shall we say, a New Heaven, and a New Earth. Stay tuned, true believers. It will all be clear in due time.

Appendix: Cthulhu

In the *Book of the SubGenius,* they say that the elder gods (or Old Ones) are not active, rather that they are "sleeping". In the courses of my coming and going, I happened to wake them up, the foremost of them being Cthulhu. I saw him in a lesser form, mostly, a man in a black robe whose head was an octopus. I dropped a rock on him once, in my visions, though I had no reason to. It seemed like the thing to do: thus my lesson to not judge something as evil too quickly. Actually, Cthulhu was always nice to me. I don't know why. It was said that the Old Ones operated outside the sphere of good and evil, but I remember him saying at one point, "If we had to choose, we would pick evil, because it would be more fun."

I saw Cthulhu in a darker form, once, and I blogged about it, from a memory from a decade before the writing:

> In any event, it happened just so: I was in Korea, back in 1994, staying at my aunt's house. I was still smoking cigarettes at the time, so I was in their garage, smoking. And I don't know who it was of the ones floating around in my head that triggered it, but I heard the sound as of a gate opening, and it was as if the veil of reality were lifting. And I remember staring at a plain, orange bicycle, and as the veil, as of the reality was uncovered what was below it, I saw the frame begin to twist out tentacles of flame, flame burning with unholy pain: the head of Cthulhu; everything around me began to unravel in hideous convulsing horror. But just for a moment, thank God in His mercy. Just as soon

as it started, it stopped, and everything was back to normal. But it was an experience I will not forget—ever. [6/28/05]

Indeed, it truly was horror that I was dealing with. But except for that one vision, all Cthulhu ever showed me was kindness. That vision in itself might have been kindness, a sort of warning. I remember when speaking of pain and the voluntary taking of pain and how we would volunteer for pain was bandied about, Cthulhu made a sharpening sound between a kitchen knife and its sharpening rod, and made as if an intent toward me as if he were going to cut me. And I got the message: pain wasn't a game. And he never did cut me.

We had some conversations, back in my days in Korea in the '90s, and it was clear that I didn't need to introduce reason to him at all. About the rock I dropped on his head, he asked why I did that. Didn't even seem to be mad at me about it. I apologized for it, and he asked me what I had awakened them for. To which I answered, "True love." They seemed keen on the idea, Cthulhu and the other Old Ones. Of course, that was during my Arquette phase, so I hadn't found it yet. They liked the look of Sin, whom they'd never seen before. They were pretty normal, all of them, though I only really talked to Cthulhu and a little to his brother, Hastur (the unspeakable).

And then years later I found that I must have made an impression on him, for he had apparently changed his mind in actually choosing a side. He found out that I was squarely on the side of good, so he chose that side to be friends with me in eternity. I even converted him to Christianity. Because of this, John the Baptist said of me that I ventured into the darkness and made friends with the horror inside. Truly, let it be a lesson to you: even Cthulhu could be reasoned with. Don't be too quick to judge.

Anyone. Even a horror can find the light. The height of madness brought down to Earth. And made right.

Endnotes

i Philip K. Dick, *Exegesis*
ii Revelation 12:4
iii E. E. Cummings, "somewhere i have never traveled, gladly beyond"
iv Steve Miller, "The Joker"
v Mark 2:27
vi Kurt Vonnegut, *Welcome to the Monkey House*
vii The Fixx, "Are We Ourselves?"
viii Jorge Luis Borges
ix Nick Drake, "Fruit Tree"
x J. K. Rowling, *Harry Potter and the Deathly Hallows*
xi Cameron Crowe, *Jerry Maguire*
xii Gavin Rossdale, "Love Remains the Same"
xiii Al Jean, *The Simpsons*
xiv Introduction, *The Six Million Dollar Man*
xv Pink Floyd, *The Wall*
xvi Stephen King, *The Shining*
xvii Tim Rice, *Evita*
xviii Luke 1:44
xix Carly Simon, "You're So Vain"
xx Francis Ford Copolla, *Apocalypse Now*
xxi Frankie Lymon, "Why Do Fools Fall in Love"
xxii Andy Wachowski & Lana Wachowski, *The Matrix*
xxiii The Who, "Love, Reign O'er Me"
xxiv Furry Lewis, "I Will Turn Your Money Green"
xxv Led Zeppelin, "Fool in the Rain"
xxvi Coldplay, "Clocks"
xxvii The Beatles, "All You Need Is Love"
xxviii Kurt Vonnegut, *Slaughterhouse Five*
xxix Philip K. Dick, *The Divine Invasion*
xxx Joseph Heller, *Catch-22*
xxxi 2 Timothy 4:7, NIV
xxxii Matthew 7:7, KJV
xxxiii Queen, "Bohemian Rhapsody"
xxxiv W. B. Yeats, "The Second Coming"
xxxv John H. Doe, *The Gospel According to Judas*

Made in the USA
Charleston, SC
30 November 2015